HOW TO SUCCEED WITHOUT A CAREER PATH

HOW TO SUCCEED WITHOUT A CAREER PATH

Jobs for People With No Corporate Ladder

Howard G. Rosenberg, Ph.D.

IMPACT PUBLICATIONS
Manassas Park, VA

HOW TO SUCCEED WITHOUT A CAREER PATH
Jobs for People With No Corporate Ladder

Library of Congress Cataloguing-in-Publication Data

Rosenberg, Howard G., 1945—
  How to succeed without a career path : jobs for people with no corporate ladder / Howard D. Rosenberg.
    p. cm.
  Includes bibliographical references and index.
  ISBN 1-57023-003-X : 13.95
  1. Vocational guidance. 2. Vocational interests. 3. Success.
I. Title.
HF5381.R762   1994
331.7'02'0973—dc20   94—457
                                                               CIP

For information on distribution or quantity discount rates, Tel. 703/361-7300, Fax 703/335-9486, or write to: Sales Department, IMPACT PUBLICATIONS, 9104-N Manassas Drive, Manassas Park, VA 22111-5211, Distributed to the trade by National Book Network, 4720 Boston Way, Suite A, Lanham, MD 20706, Tel. 301/459-8696 or 800/462-6420.

CONTENTS

INTRODUCTION

*T*he beaches of Southern California bring out strange and creative ideas. One of those ideas is that our society has gone too far in emphasizing the importance of careers. As evidence of this, there are hundreds of books available to teach you how to choose, change and advance your career. Advice on resume writing, interviewing, job seeking, networking, and cover letters is abundantly available. You could spend the next two years reading these publications and never find a satisfying life.

This book is different. It will help you assess and develop your entire life, not just your career, and redefine the importance of work. Put aside all preconceived notions about the importance of careers and focus on your life. This is an opportunity for a new beginning. What is your role in this development? You must take this book seriously and complete the recommended exercises described within. Also, you must take these concepts several steps further and read recommended publications. And finally, you need to share your goals and dreams with significant others in your life. Increased success in your life and work awaits if you do all of this. I cannot promise you an always beautiful life but personal balance and contentment will increase.

The ideas in this book have been discussed with hundreds of people and almost everyone wants to know how quickly they can get a copy.

That convinces me this book deals with an important need within individuals: how to feel good about yourself without having to develop a fast moving career. Are these individuals appeasing me or are they different from other people? I doubt it. A sincere thanks to all of you who have provided me with ideas. A special thanks to Sandra Hagevick for constant inspiration and ideas.

1

DO YOU NEED A CAREER TO FEEL SUCCESSFUL?

*C*areer, career, career. That is a word we hear quite often. Doctors and lawyers have careers. Criminals have careers. Students in higher education have college careers, and some make a career out of going to college. In our society, careers are unfortunately often equated with success. Among the first questions asked at social gatherings, is "what do you do?" Our identities have been trapped into our careers, as we forget about individual values, personal development, and helping others.

THE RISE OF CAREERISM

In the years before 1940, there were very few careers and people had jobs. Shortly after World War II, "careerism" emerged. The GI bill allowed more people to go to college than ever before. Higher education expanded rapidly and graduates found a multitude of opportunities in engineering, business, science, education, the arts, and other fields. Major corporations expanded their work forces and could not find enough college graduates. Technological advances demanded a highly educated work force. Additionally, the media in the 1950's and 1960's portrayed highly successful lawyers and doctors with their large offices, high salaries, beautiful homes and prestige. Parents saw these images and saved endlessly to give their children a college education. The option of

1

not attending college was eliminated for many children and it was professionalism or being disowned. Sometimes children inherited career baggage and were asked to obtain career successes that parents never obtained.

As indicated in Chart 1, the 1970's and 1980's showed a continued expansion of career opportunities in our country and abroad. Computer personnel, accountants, engineers and many other professionals were in great demand. There were many more positions than qualified candidates. In 1982 there were 142 new jobs for every one hundred college graduates. By 1993 the numbers had dropped dramatically and there were only 16 new jobs for every one hundred college students.

CHART 1
GROWTH OF CAREERS AND PEOPLE
ENTERING THE LABOR MARKET

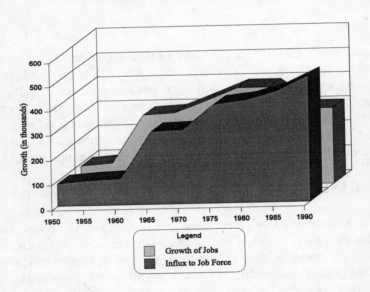

Legend
Growth of Jobs
Influx to Job Force

Today there are fifty million more people working than in 1970, which is difficult for our economy to absorb. This twenty-four-year growth equals the entire growth for the previous seventy years.

Unexpectedly, the 1980's and 1990's have shown a dramatic reversal in career opportunities. Massive layoffs have occurred with professionals no longer exempt. The demand for highly trained employees has diminished. Engineers, computer analysts and managers now find jobs difficult to obtain. What has happened to all of the work that was once available? Some manufacturers have decided it is cheaper to buy materials, particularly from third world nations, than produce them. Machinery has continued to replace lower skilled workers. Consultants and specialists are being hired more for brief assignments rather than as permanent employees. Also, middle management positions are being eliminated and remaining managers are being given responsibilities for several departments. *Time Magazine* recently told the story very vividly: "White collar layoffs are permanent and structural. These jobs are gone forever." New positions opening up are in the $5 to $9 range. Bellboys now have bachelor's degrees.

CAREER INSECURITY

Careers provided a great deal of security, a basic human need, in our society for approximately forty years. The next twenty years will show a swing in the opposite direction. Ask engineers, sales people, stock brokers, professional athletes, computer personnel, recreational workers and others how much job security they have and the response will be none to moderate. This is a fact with which we have to learn to live. Long term work commitments and contracts are history. On the other hand, relying on other areas of our life to provide security will be increasingly important in years to come. Those areas include family, health, financial planning, friendships, geographical location, and spirituality. More men than ever are seeking psychological counseling to help with this transition. Also, increasing numbers of mothers and fathers are decreasing work commitments to be at home with young children. The lists below compare security sources in the past and in the present and future.

SECURITY 1950-1989

Career, 60-70%
Family, 10-20%
Friends, 10-20%
Spirituality, 5-15%

SECURITY 1990-2010

Career, 20-40%
Family, 20-30%
Friends, 10-20%
Financial,
   planning 10-20%
Health, 10%
Spirituality 10-20%
Interpersonal and
   adaptive skills 20-30%

Newspapers and magazines are filled with articles describing employment difficulties of new and experienced workers. The worst employment picture in thirty-five years for college graduates is how this period is being characterized. So, how have people adjusted to these changes? Look around and you will see that the changing job demographics are being ignored. College students are seeking careers in greater numbers than ever before. Law schools and MBA programs have grown tremendously. Women have jumped on the corporate ladder in search of a prestigious career. The employment picture has changed a great deal, but our way of thinking and behaving is the same as thirty years ago? People think and act as if there are no options to success other than having a professional career and furthermore, that they will obtain one. "The current business definition of success, which is always being ahead of where you were before, must change," says Margaret Henning, Dean of Simmons College Graduate School of Management in Boston. According to Henning, success is "setting your own definition of success, controlling it and having choices. It means balancing work and family, personal and professional, and having a quality life."

If you have planned most of your life to have a successful career, it will probably be very difficult to release these expectations and feel good about yourself if you choose to deviate from your prior expectations. Many years, thousands of dollars, and high parental expectations may influence your career preparation. Parents are very concerned about the success of their children, sometimes to their detriment. In talking with parents over the years, it has become apparent that they are most concerned about their children finding careers that provide very good employment opportunities and above average pay. Usually of secondary importance were careers in which their children would find self-fulfillment. It is easy to understand why so many people make career changes since their first career choice was so highly influenced by parents' wishes. Research has shown that parental expectations are highly correlated with self esteem and career choice.

ADULT CHILDREN OF WORKAHOLICS

A great deal has been written in the last few years about adult children of alcoholics but little about children whose parents were workaholics. Many of the some dynamics and issues occur in both groups. Children of workaholics rarely feel good about themselves unless they are working. What caused their parents to become workaholics? Many of them grew up in the post depression/post World War II era. During this era people feared not having enough work, food and clothing to survive. Receiving psychotherapy to deal with these fears was rare. Also, immediately after World War II business and career opportunities began to expand rapidly. Small businesses could be started with $2500-3000. Colleges and professional schools were easy to enter. America, the world leader had 75% of the world's gross national product. For individuals who were willing to work hard the rewards came quickly and many fortunes were made.

Children were given very mixed messages. On one hand their parents worked very hard, and their children observed this. On the other hand the children were given many material rewards that they had not earned. Parents put a great deal of pressure on their children to achieve in school and work, but gave them rewards regardless. As competition grew for admission into college, children were not ready for the increased sacrifices needed for success. They entered college and the work force and tried to achieve a great deal, but competition and lack of opportunities made it impossible to obtain to their parents level.

Recalling these childhood pressures and discussing them with your parents or siblings can help you gain more control over your life. Additionally, we often choose as mates individuals who bring up these same conflicts because we are trying to resolve them.

When you were growing up, what kind of verbal and non-verbal messages did your parents give about the following occupations:

	OK to Pursue	**Not OK to Pursue**
truck driver		
lawyer		
cook		
postal employee		
teacher		
airline pilot		
recreation supervisor		
accountant		
medical doctor		
salesperson		
gardener		
taxi driver		
sales clerk		

What did your siblings, relatives and friends think about the occupations listed above? Were they also influenced by their parents about occupations to pursue. What would your elementary and high school teachers think about the occupations listed above? Did they subtlety influence your career direction, while talking positively about some occupations and ignoring others?

Can you see a pattern here? Most young children are highly influenced in career directions without an opportunity to understand them. Students have already made conscious or unconscious career decisions without ever experiencing work. Many college students think they will become vice-presidents of an organization within five years.

Consider how your education prepared you for specific occupations. Were you trained for an engineering or technical position? Were you ever told that the work force needs are always changing and you should be prepared for these changes? How did your first work experiences influence your career? Like most people, did you feel slightly inadequate and obtain more education in your field? Can you see how this invested you further in one direction? How does your family currently influence your career options? What type of work would you feel comfortable telling your family that you do? How does your lifestyle influence your options? What material comforts do you have as a result of your occupation? How does your knowledge of careers influence your options? Can you see how all of these influences have had a powerful impact on your choice of a career. We are often led down a path with having only a limited choice of which path to choose. Once we have started down this path, it is difficult to change directions, particularly on our own.

Due to company layoffs, Mark Thompson a 43 year old engineer has just lost his second job in three years. Nine months ago, Ann Clark graduated from college with a degree in finance and has had only one job interview. After eight years of full time parenting, Marsha Simpson is trying to reenter the job market and is finding only low paying service jobs. Michelle Gordon has been laid off as Vice-President of advertising after her company hired an outside agency to handle this function. Are any of these stories familiar to you?

Have you recently lost your job or know of others who did? Perhaps you have just graduated from college and cannot find promising opportunities? Maybe you feel stuck because your career is not advancing? Perhaps you do not even want a career but feel like an outcast if you do not pursue one. These situations today are unfortunately very common and may result in one of the most difficult and frustrating periods of your life. You may be blaming yourself for making bad academic and career choices, even though at the time you were doing what seemed best.

If you are feeling a great deal of depression, sadness, frustration or anger about your career, short term supportive counseling can be very helpful. Talking with a professional psychologist or counselor every one or two weeks for a month or two can make this period of your life much easier. Less expensive resources available include local mental health centers, churches, YWCA's and YMCA's, and college counseling centers.

Other ways to deal with this difficult period in your life include increasing your exercise, talking to friends about concerns, joining a support group, and developing other areas of your life. Keeping your stress level as low as possible is important. Some helpful books include:

When Smart People Fail by Carole Hyatt and Linda Gottlieb

The Road Less Traveled by M. Scott Peck

Anger: How to Live With and Without it by Albert Ellis

Whatever you do, please be kind with yourself. I know you are trying to correct the situation so try not to demean or criticize yourself. This will only make the situation worse. Give yourself positive strokes for trying hard and reassure yourself that things will change. You have succeeded in many ways so reflect on those successes and remind yourself that good times will return.

Individuals with slowly advancing careers usually go through several stages which include:

1. Denial that their career is not advancing or that they will not find satisfying employment;

2. Attempts to overcome being stuck by attending seminars to increase their motivation or skills in a specific area;

3. Frustration because of inability to find employment or advance;

4. Blaming others such as older employees or the economy for their frustrations and inability to advance;

5. Seeking unnecessary career changes even though they enjoy their work;

6. Accepting their situation, seeing the positive sides, and improving their current work situation with additional tasks;

7. Finding success in rewarding activities outside of their work.

Learning From Others

We can learn a great deal from retired people. These individuals have no fast paced advancing career but are usually happy with their life. Retired people have learned to find satisfaction in other areas of their lives including family, free time, recreation and travel, to name a few. Amazingly, another group to learn from is people who have lost their eyesight. Usually blind people have difficulty adjusting at first. Later they learn to cherish their hearing, tasting, smelling and kinesthetic senses. Life goes on for them and with the help of friends, remains very satisfying. Talk to a blind person and you will be see how they have adapted.

Similar to blind people, individuals without rapidly advancing careers need to develop other areas of their lives.

What Else Did You Learn From Your Education in Addition to Career Preparation?

College students frequently feel that their education has not been worthwhile if a high paying job is not found. Higher education provides many skills including:

- Analytical reasoning ability
- Verbal and written communication skills
- Human relations and interpersonal skills
- Research and investigative ability
- Learning skills
- Cultural diversity awareness
- Leadership skills

These skills can be used in a variety of positions and occupations including management, sales, research, teaching, science, counseling, and parenting.

Career Reality

Professionals in all fields will admit their work has both positive and negative sides. If careers are going well, good salaries, advancement, and opportunities to use special abilities are provided. Quite often though, the reality is that careers have ups and downs and usually are not as glamorous, or self-fulfilling as we imagine. A nursing administrator recently admitted to me that she felt uncomfortable telling her daughter how wonderful careers are while returning from work everyday both tired and frustrated. Frequently there are aspects of the work that are not particularly enjoyable but have to be completed. Budgets, annual reports and other paperwork can cure the worst cases of sleeplessness. Additional negative effects of high stress careers include health problems such as high blood pressure, insomnia and heart attacks. Psychological problems caused by high stress careers include lack of self-esteem, depression and marital problems.

In a recent nationwide poll conducted for the Shearson Lehman Brothers by the Roper Organization, 45 percent of adults said they would choose a different career if they could start over. *Money Magazine* in November, 1992 rated one hundred occupations on a variety of factors including personal satisfaction. Only twenty four occupations received a satisfaction rating of good or excellent. Most people rated their satisfaction as average, fair or poor including teachers, computer analysts, financial planners and advertising executives. The satisfaction rating was the same for homemakers as accountants! Regardless of this information, people pursue careers as if they will provide endless positive rewards.

CAREER MYTHS AND REALITIES

Myth 1:   **Careers start at age 21-25 and continue to age 60-65.**

Reality: Careers can start at age 21, 30, 39, 44, 53, 60 and other times. They stop and start over again many, many times during our life.

Myth 2:   **Everyone with a college education will have a career.**

Reality: The number of career opportunities are decreasing in the

United States. Only 20% of new jobs will require a college education.

Myth 3:   **Career choices are separate from personal growth.**

Reality: Your career and personal life are intimately intermingled.

Myth 4:   **If you work hard at finding a professional job, you will likely obtain one.**

Reality: Hard work alone is not enough. You may spend hundreds of hours job seeking and end up in a very compromised situation.

Myth 5:   **There is a "right" career for everyone.**

Reality: Most people can succeed in and enjoy a variety of careers.

Myth 6:   **Once a career position is obtained a great deal of satisfaction will follow.**

Reality: Many people make career changes frequently due to lack of satisfaction.

Myth 7:   **Changing careers is a sign of confusion.**

Reality: Changing careers is a normal developmental process because our needs and values change over time.

Myth 8:   **Organizations are looking for dedicated, career-oriented employees.**

Reality: Organizations are hiring temporary and part-time employees to fill 50 percent of their openings.

Myth 9:   **The economy will rebound and there will be numerous career opportunities.**

Reality: The economy may rebound but organizations will continue downsizing and hiring temporary employees.

Myth 10: **Advanced degrees will improve job opportunities.**

Reality: Regardless of degrees, unemployment will remain high.

Myth 11: **People have a great deal of control over their career and can shape their direction.**

Reality: Most careers are a compromise between what you desire and what is expected by your employer, supervisor, family, health, or other obligations.

Helpful Advice?

Recently, the director of a placement office in a small college gave the following advice to graduating seniors who were job seeking:

Salary: "Be very flexible in negotiations."

Benefits: "With companies on tight budgets, don't expect a lot."

Geography: "Be ready to move and settle for a job that is not in your dream city."

Job responsibilities: "Be willing to accept non-glamorous ones, pay your dues and prove yourself."

Work hours: "Be prepared to work long hours."

Are careers really worth the great sacrifice that is suggested here? How many personal needs must be ignored? Is there any guarantee that these compromises are temporary and will be obtained later.

JOB OR CAREER: WHICH IS BEST FOR YOU?

It may be difficult for you to determine if a career or non-career job would be best for you. The questionnaire below can help you make this decision. If you are not currently employed, answer the questions based upon previous employment or how you would respond if working.

		YES	NO
1.	When someone asks you "how things are going" do you talk first about your job?	____	____
2.	Do you think about your work a lot when you are at home?	____	____
3.	Do you often work at home in the evenings or weekends?	____	____
4.	Do you actively participate in professional associations related to your work?	____	____
5.	Do you often read professional articles related to your work?	____	____
6.	Do you often go to work early and stay late?	____	____
7.	Frequently, do you work through the lunch hour?	____	____
8.	Do you usually seek additional responsibilities at work?	____	____
9.	Are your work accomplishments more rewarding than personal growth or family achievements?	____	____
10.	Are you continuously seeking to upgrade your work skills?	____	____
11.	Do you envy others in high level positions?	____	____
	Totals	____	____

As you can infer from this questionnaire, careers imply a unique commitment to work. This means many extra hours thinking, preparing and working. Careerists also participate in professional organizations and often seek additional responsibilities at work.

If you answered "Yes" ten times, and enjoy your work, you definitely want a career and this book may be inappropriate for you at this time. If you had the same but do not enjoy your work, read on. Answering "Yes" between seven and nine times indicates mixed career ambitions. If you answered "Yes" six or fewer times, this is the book for you. There is new hope for your successful non-career future. Come along with me on this journey and you will discover more success than you ever dreamed of having.

References

Anger: How to Live With and Without it. Albert Ellis. Carol Publishing, 1992.

Depression and its Treatment. John Greist and James Jefferson. Warner Books, 1984.

Forty Something. Ross Goldstein. Tarcher Press, 1990.

How to Survive Trauma. Benjamen Colodzin. Olympia Institute, 1993.

Money Magazine, November, 1992.

The Encouragement Book. Don Dinkmeyer and L. Losong. Fireside Books, 1992.

The Healing Power of Humor. Allen Klein. Tarcher Perigree Books, 1989.

The Road Less Traveled. M. Scott Peck. Simon & Schuster, 1978.

What Smart People Do When They Lose Their Jobs. Kathleen A. Riehle. John Wiley & Sons, 1993.

When Smart People Fail. Carole Hyatt and Linda Gottlieb. Penguin Books, 1993.

2

MAINTAINING CONTROL OVER YOUR CAREER

P restige, challenge, and monetary reward can come from successful careers. Careers can also bring disappointment frustration, burnout, lack of self esteem, divorce and even suicide. As evidence of disappointment, increasing numbers of executives are trading in the corporate rat race for work that they love. Former executive Karen Hilburn "dropped out" of corporate America to pursue her exotic dream, living and working on a private yacht in St. Maarten. Two and one half years later she basks in warm trade winds that have taken her to exotic ports of call throughout the Caribbean, South America and Italy. Her 9 to 5 workday is a far cry from the 16 hour days she racked up as a coordinator during the "Perry Mason" television series. "These have been the best two years of my life," she said.

What happened to those fulfilling careers that we strived hard to reach and spent endless time and energy developing? How did they become so frustrating? Were they just an illusion? Several factors contribute to making a careers difficult.

- We did not realize the competition from others in accomplishing our goals. Many more people are competing for fewer quality positions than ever before.

- We took on too much responsibility. Until security is reached within an organization, people take as much responsibility as possible. Yes, this does increase the chances of keeping a job, but it also accelerates burnout.

- Along with too much responsibility, having too many employees to supervise can cause burnout, particularly with the "me generation." High achievers are a delight to supervise but usually do not stay long in one position. Low achievers, particularly ones that get sick on a regular basis or forget to do their work on time, put great strain on managers, but often are not easy to fire.

- Climbing the corporate ladder and obtaining an impressive title and job with high responsibility and visibility can lead to difficulties. Many people burn out from these positions due to public scrutiny and pressure.

- Living in an information rich and rapidly changing world is exciting. Research and journal articles are available on any topic. Staying current with all of this new information and change though is problematic and adds pressure to our work. Wouldn't you love to have time to read two new articles a week?

- Professional associations rely on volunteers for direction but an enormous amount of time is needed for those leadership positions. Anything over two hours a week can have a negative effect on your lifestyle.

- Is time really shrinking or is it just an illusion that there were 24 hours in a day. It takes more time every year to get the same thing done at the same speed. Professional careers demand increasing amounts of time each year.

- No society in the history of the world is as process oriented and has as many meetings as the U.S. As Total Quality Management spreads, the number of meetings has dramatically increased. What would happen if there was a one year moratorium on meetings?

a. People would get 30% more work done
b. People would get 50% more work done
c. The quality of work would be decreased
d. The quality of work would be increased
e. People would know less
f. People would know more
g. Employees would feel left out of decisions
h. Employees would feel overjoyed

Meetings do serve a purpose of informing others (which could be done by electronic mail), getting input (usually only from the most verbal people) and consensus decision making (because no one wants to take responsibility for a bad decision).

■ Working in a pressure cooker. These days many organizations are having financial problems and employees are asked to do a great deal more with fewer resources. In some companies the success of one product may mean the difference between life or death of the organization.

■ Some problems are unsolvable, given the amount of available resources. Other times problems can be solved but only against the wishes of a group of people. Make sure the problem can be solved before volunteering to take it on, or you set yourself up for failure.

TALKING TO YOUR CAREER

When was the last time you had a heart to heart discussion with your career? You have discussions with your children, spouse, and fellow workers, then why not your career? The "empty chair" technique can be particularly useful in this conversation. Arrange two chairs face to face about three feet apart. One chair is for your career and the other for you.

Sit in your career chair first and tell yourself (in the other chair) how your career is going? Some statements your career might make are:

"I am really bored, what can you do to change me."

"This past year was really great, thanks for looking after me."

"You need to take it easier on me, I am exhausted."

"Something is missing in my daily activities and I do not know what."

"You have been goofing off the last two years and I am getting bored. Can you put more energy into me?"

"I am ready for a change."

"You used to love me and now I feel like I am being ignored."

Next, go over and sit in the other chair and respond to the statements your career just made. Some responses might be:

"You are right, I am not putting as much time as I used to into you."

The conversation might continue. . .

Career Chair:	"So what are you going to do about it?"
You:	"I am not sure. Do you have any suggestions?"
Career Chair:	"Yes, I am glad you asked. I would like for you to try two or three new ways to energize me. One thing would be to quit this company. Another is to learn better computer skills. How does this sound to you?"
You:	"I would like to put you back in the closet with all the other chairs."
Career Chair:	"You have the power to do that but you know I will be back sooner or later. Besides, have you noticed how crowded it is getting in that closet with all of your other chairs?"
You:	"You are right. I need to listen to you but I do not want to try two or three new career activities. I have a new child that I want to spend time with."
Career Chair:	"Would you consider one new activity?"

| You: | "Yes, I was thinking about taking a class on communication skills. This would help me at work and with my family." |

| Career Chair: | "Now we are talking." |

Continue this dialogue until you and your career agree on what to do next. You may decide to take a leave of absence, change organizations or move to a different city.

| Career Chair: | "I have been with this organization for five years and I am getting bored." |

| You: | "So am I but you know how hard it is to find work." |

| Career Chair: | "You have not even tried. It may not be as difficult as you think." |

| You: | "What would you suggest?" |

| Career Chair: | "Update your resume and send it to a few places. Also start inquiring informally about the situation in other organizations. Take it slowly but work on it." |

| You: | "Good idea; just take it slowly." |

| Career Chair: | "Yes, that's all I'm asking, but it will make me feel better." |

CHANGING YOUR CURRENT JOB

Perhaps you are in a job that cannot be easily discarded because you are close to retirement or do not want to lose your benefits. Maybe you enjoy where you live or your family would be upset if you suggested major changes. Modifying your current job may be the best option at this time. What are some potential ways to accomplish this?

Reorganize, Refurnish or Move Your Office

Cleaning out file cabinets, drawers, and closets can give an uplift similar to losing weight. Bringing in new pictures, lamps and other furniture can give a "new job" feeling.

Teach Others What You Know

Contact your company training and development department, local high school or college and volunteer to teach a seminar or class. Training programs look for individuals who can present new ideas and teachers love to find individuals who will present current information.

Join or Develop an Informal Support Network in Your Organization

These networks discuss work problems or broader social issues (e.g. womens' or minority networks).

Analyze Your Current Position and Decide Which Parts Are Least Desirable, Then Find Someone Who Would Enjoy Doing It

Other people are often bored with their jobs and would like new challenges, if approached correctly. First, decide who might be interested. Talk with the person and discuss the importance of the work. Next show them they have the skills to do the work and agree to provide additional training. Third, help them with any problems and publicize the fact that they are taking on new responsibilities. Add pay or other incentives if possible.

Train an Intern From a Local High School or College

Many young people are eager to learn new skills in the work place. They bring an eagerness that will revitalize other employees. Often students will work for little or no pay, just for the experience and opportunity to test out an occupation. To find interns, contact your local high school guidance office or college career services/internship program. Helping develop students' new work and social skills can be a very rewarding experience.

Find Volunteers to Work in Your Office

If you prefer to work with older individuals, many retired people will volunteer their time. Retired professionals feel lost without work and people contact and bring experience and skills that are an excellent asset. Contact your local community volunteer agency for referrals.

Seth, a retired vice president for operations from a manufacturing organization was sitting at home very bored and feeling that he was wasting his many years of experience. He investigated volunteer work in several agencies but could not quite find the right fit. Seth approached the career center at a major university and volunteered to critique students' resumes. Over the years he has seen thousands of resumes and was particularly familiar with the engineering field, an area in which other staff had limited knowledge. Seth loved the work, found it very easy and helped many students.

Attend Seminars and Workshops or Out of Town Conferences

We all love to learn particularly when it enriches our work. Numerous seminars are available on work related topics. Try to attend these workshops at least once every two months.

Connie was a very bright office assistant for a chemical products distributor, but lacked computer experience. She found an organization that gave one day seminars on word processing and programming and learned skills that enabled her to obtain a promotion.

Volunteer for Fun Committees at Work

There are always some committees in every organization that need assistance. This is an excellent way to meet people from other departments and help with problems. Volunteering will also help your reputation and may lead to other benefits. Make sure the committees are not drudgery or focused on unsolvable issues.

Mary worked in payroll for six years at a major pharmaceutical firm. Although she enjoyed the work, it gave her minimal contact with people. Volunteering for the Employee Development Task Force gave her several new friends and a great deal of knowledge about the organization.

Start an Office Sports Team

Organizations realize the importance of having recreation for their employees but often do not have resources to develop them. Organizing a team can boost morale, promote networking with other departments, and develop new friendships.

Karen was bored one winter and convinced five people from her office to join the company bowling league. Their team was awful, finishing last in nearly every match. One night the team caught fire and bowled the high series for that year. Karen was asked later if she would like to chair the bowling league, which of course she refused.

Join Professional Associations Without Taking On Leadership Roles

Professional associations are an excellent way to network for jobs, discover how other organizations deal with problems, make friends and develop new skills. Make sure the organization does not ask more than it gives.

Conduct an Analysis Among Several Organizations of Similar Problems

Take the initiative and contact people who might have ideas that can improve your organization or the professional field. You can become an expert and often these results can be published in newsletters or journals.

Making Work Less Stressful

If you cannot change work then it is wise to reduce the stress and maintain energy for outside accomplishments. Some ways to decrease stress are:

- **Wear Less Formal Clothes.** Some organizations are very formal in their dress codes, others are more casual. Try dressing as comfortably as possible to reduce stress.

- **Exercise During the Lunch Hour.** Getting away for an hour and exercising will reduce stress and make it easier to complete work in the afternoon. If vigorous exercise is not possible go for a walk or visit a museum.

- **Ask for Help.** Everyone needs help during high stress periods. Make sure that you reciprocate during co-workers' stressful times.

- **Just Say No.** If you do not have the time, energy or interest, tell the person making the request you cannot help. Be honest and agree to help them at some other time.

- **Play Soft Music in Your Office.** Playing music can provide buoyancy to your work day and make your job less stressful.

- **Put Plants in Your Office.** Greenery can give you a feeling that you are outside, another stress reducer for most people.

- **Close the Door and Do Not Answer the Phone.** Decreasing the number of interruptions can provide the time to complete tasks that could take forever. Small five minute tasks can be done at the end of the day, so save major time for major projects.

- **Take Vacations and Mental Health Days.** Stress can be significantly reduced by taking short vacations and staying at home when you are very tired. Try to take these mental health breaks once a month.

3

DEFINING YOUR OWN SUCCESS

A few years ago, on a visit to California, I took an enjoyable sailboat cruise of the Santa Barbara harbor. The captain of the sailboat described his former career as an advertising executive for a large organization in Minneapolis. A great deal of pressure and many twelve hour work days came with this position. After several years of this demanding work, he took a vacation to Santa Barbara and realized that one of his major enjoyments in life, sailing, had been greatly neglected. Also he discovered that no one was conducting sailing tours of the Santa Barbara harbor. Shortly after returning to Minneapolis he took a leave of absence from his job, moved to Santa Barbara, bought a sailboat for less than $10,000 and started his tours. His advertising and public relations background helped develop the business to the point that he makes more money now than in his previous position. Which job do you think he enjoys more? Remaining a sailboat tour director forever is not his goal, but for the moment his work is very satisfying and the first step toward self fulfillment.

LEARN FROM YOUR
SUCCESSES AND FAILURES

Everyone would love to be successful easily and have their life filled with a wonderful family, a good job, many friends and good health; with little or no effort. The second best scenario would be to succeed based upon hard work. The worst situation is to fail after working hard, which usually leads to frustration, depression and lowered expectations. Review the past several years and look at what you:

- Achieved easily,
- Achieved with work,
- Have not achieved with work,
- Have given up on.

What have you learned from both your successes and failures?

CHARACTERISTICS OF SUCCESSFUL PEOPLE

It may be hard to believe, but many successful, happy and wonderful people are not presidents, vice-presidents or directors in their organizations. They do not have huge houses or brand new cars, yet they consider themselves successful. These individuals have a different measure of success. They are successful because they:

- **Maintain a Positive Attitude.** Successful people do not suffer from attitudinal sclerosis and become set in their own ways. They are constantly seeing the positive side of life and therefore minor setbacks are seen as just that.

- **Keep a Balance in Their Lives.** If you look at the work schedule of "successful people" you will see that they do not work hard all day long. Successful people have plenty of time for family and neighborhood causes. Their identity is not defined in their career.

- **Have a Great Deal of Self Control Delay Gratification.** In our instant gratification society, people expect to become rich and famous very quickly. Successful people are able to put off immediate rewards for long range goals. For example, they eat and drink moderately which keeps their energy level high. What does this behavior do for them? It gives them a sense of control over their lives.

- **Know Their Strengths and Weaknesses.** Everyone has strengths and weaknesses. Successful people not only know what their skills are but also know when and how to use each. They usually use strengths in difficult situations and ask for help or try to improve in weak areas.

- **Enjoy Their Work.** Successful people enjoy their work successes without considering advancement. Their work gives them a great sense of satisfaction and reward.

- **Have Alternate Plans in Case the Original Does Not Work.** The Johnson family started a small manufacturing company and needed a new building. They built a structure without walls so that if the business failed the building could be converted into a comfortable home. We need to have alternate plans and be prepared for the unexpected.

- **Are Involved in Several Interests at Once.** Successful people do not put all of their eggs in one basket, whether it be friendships, work or hobbies. Why do they behave this way? First of all they have many interests and a great deal of energy. Secondly, they have learned not to rely on one activity or person to provide all of their needs for feeling good.

- **Know What They Want and Move Towards it.** If you do not know what is important to you, chances are excellent that you will never obtain it. Successful people have a clear picture of what is important to them. They may not know exactly how to get there and sometimes face setbacks, but they continue to work towards their goal without losing sight of it.

- **Experiment with Options.** If you are fixing something and your solution is not working, try something different. Sometimes the most obvious solution to a problem does not work. Unsuccessful people continue to try the same approach, only harder. Successful people often try something very different even if it does not make sense. Trying unique options has solved many problems and created major advances in science, medicine and social service.

- **Help Others with Their Personal and Social Problems.** Successful people obtain a great deal of satisfaction from helping others during difficult times. The rewards they obtain fill the bank accounts of their heart.

- **Dress and Groom Themselves Very Nicely.** How do many successful people stand out in a crowd; by their dressing and grooming habits. They do not always have the latest clothing and jewelry but they do have high quality and wear it well. They keep their clothing and appearance very tidy and well cared for. This of course shows a great deal of pride in themselves.

- **Have Control over Their Careers Not the Opposite.** Do you ever feel that your career is the most demanding thing in your life? It requires constant feeding, nurturing, training and retraining, and endless amount of time and energy. Successful people have control over their careers which allows them to seek and obtain many rewards outside of their work.

- **Are Sensitive Listeners.** High quality listening is quickly becoming a lost skill in our society. Individuals are so busy and wrapped up in their own needs that they do not hear what other people are saying. By listening, not only to words but also to feelings, we can make friends, help others, obtain assistance and learn a great deal without pain. The next time you interact with someone, try not to think about what you are going to say, just listen as deeply and sensitively as possible.

- **Value What They Do.** Successful people build up in importance their family, work, health, and self esteem. Unsuccessful people demean the importance of those areas.

- **Constantly Learn New Ideas, Information and Skills.** One of the great gifts given human beings is the capacity to learn. Successful people love to learn about music, computers, people, investments, gardening, health, other cultures, or many other areas. They do this by reading, taking classes, attending seminars, listening to tapes, traveling, and other methods.

- **Develop Themselves Emotionally and Spiritually.** In the everyday routine of life our emotional and personal growth is often put on the back burner. We rarely reflect on our day and review our emotions to situations encountered. It is difficult to grow as a person until we can see and understand why we reacted as we did. Think about yourself in the last week and reflect on the time you felt:

- Angry
- Rushed
- Frustrated
- Bored
- Lonely
- Depressed
- Happy
- Playful
- Witty
- Creative

- **Travel a Great Deal.** Traveling adds many benefits to our life. It relaxes us, gets our minds off of unimportant worries, helps gain a new perspective, and promotes learning. Successful people have traveling as a necessity in their lives, not a luxury, and know how to do it economically. When was the last time you took a long trip?

- **Control Their Spending.** Often success is equated with the size of the home you own or expense of your car. Most successful people do not own more house than they need. Why is this? They realize that time and expenses of owning too large a home will diminish their ability to become successful in other areas of their life. Their homes are comfortable but not extravagant. Successful people do not purchase expensive automobiles or clothes every year. What do successful people spend their money on; travel, learning, children, hobbies and personal growth.

- **Participate in Leisure Activities**. Leisure is the great release and relief in our lives, but can be easily overlooked. Often we turn our leisure into work and therefore lose the renewal aspect of it. Successful people have leisure as a part of each day, even if it is only for a few minutes.

- **Take Pride in Their Families.** There is great joy in spending time with your family. Many "yuppies" now realize that rewards from helping their children grow far outweighs monetary gain at work. What help could your family use from you today ?

- **Develop and Nurture Friendships.** Friendships usually do not just happen. They need time and energy to develop. Successful people have many friends with whom they share both enjoyable and difficult times and also several upbeat people that bring new energy into their life. Every good friend you have will save you at least $1,000 a year. This savings comes from lower entertainment costs, assistance in repairing, vacation homes that they will let you use, free counseling they will provide, and loaned tools.

- **Stay Physically Fit and Healthy.** Physical health is taken for granted until we lose it. Many wealthy people pay a lot of money to get their health back. How is your physical health? How many hours a week do you spend to maintain and develop your health? How about your diet? How often do you eat healthy foods? What is your healthy: non-healthy food ratio? What should you eat more and less of?

- **Maintain Their Sense of Humor.** Life is serious enough without our making it worse, therefore we need to maintain our sense of humor. How can you do this if you are unemployed? Participate in humorous activities such as movies, reading the comics, doing something silly and look for the humorous things in life.

Self Esteem

If you were recently laid off from work or are having problems finding employment, chances are that your self esteem is low. This is a normal reaction to rejection and one that fortunately is temporary. Self esteem is built upon how you look, your micro and macro accomplishments, and the achievements of significant others such as your spouse or children. Knowing this we can improve our self esteem without ever finding paid employment.

Appearance. How do you feel about the way you look? Physical appearance does affect the way we feel about ourselves and how other people interact with us. Go into a store dressed nicely and you will get a different response from salespeople than if you were dressed sloppily. The same applies in work situations, at social events, or while traveling. Particularly during this difficult period of your life it helps to look better. Robert had been unemployed for six months and found very few openings in his field of teaching. The next time I saw Robert he proudly showed me his new pair of shoes which cost over $200. At first I could not understand how he could spend that much money while he was not working but later realized that the purchase boosted his self esteem. Six weeks later Robert found a teaching position.

If you have nice clothes, wear them more often, during this period. If you need to purchase quality clothes, find a discount store that sells them at reasonable prices. Also make sure that your clothes are neat and clean and take pride in how you look.

Small Achievements. Okay, so you do not have a rapidly advancing career. There are plenty of areas in your life to find success and achievement. Shall I list a few?

1. Clean out your storage area or basement.
2. Clean out your closets.
3. Clean out your car.
4. Repair something around the house.
5. Clean up your house.
6. Paint or wallpaper a room
7. Balance your checkbook or learn how.
8. Build a bookshelf.
9. Read a book that looks appealing.
10. Learn how to dance.

Can you think of three small achievements to work on now that will boost your self-esteem?

Other Self-Esteem Builders:

1. Discard the myth of perfection.
2. Never compare yourself with others.
3. Keep a written list of all your accomplishments.
4. Spend time with a friend who cares about you.
5. Give yourself time to feel good when you reach an objective.
6. List all of the things in your life for which you are grateful.
7. Sign up for a fun class.

8. Take care of yourself.
9. Keep in social circulation.

Discovering Your Own Success

Can you remember a time in the past few years when you had an accomplishment that felt wonderful? Reflect on that success for a few minutes. Chances are excellent that you have many successes in your life. Surviving in our complex society requires knowing and achieving a great deal. Unfortunately many people are not satisfied with previous successes and are always looking for new accomplishments.

If your career aspirations are not moving as quickly as you would like, forget about them and concentrate on your life. Many people assume that life should progress in a linear, progressive fashion.

One day during a meeting I was looking at a picture gallery of previous presidents of our university. In the last sixteen years there had been six individuals who held that prestigious position which meant they lasted an average of less than three years. One had retired, two went on to better jobs, one went to a different job and two returned to teaching. This pretty well summarizes life; two up, two down and two lateral. Some years we are moving ahead at a rapid pace, some years at a slow pace and other years are static. Look at the past fifteen to twenty years of your life and chart your growth on a piece of paper. To the right of each year place a dot (•) to reflect your level of perceived growth (from "Static" to "High Growth"). Join each dot with a line.

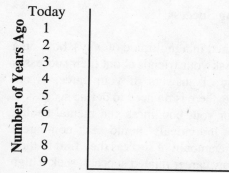

Degree of Growth

■ *Static* means you did not learn much that year and watched a lot of T.V. or similar activities.

- *Slow Growth* means you learned and did a few new things, maybe took a class or two, work and life improved slightly.
- *Moderate Growth* means you received a promotion at work and/ or took some strides in your personal development.
- *High Growth* means you earned your degree, got married or divorced, and found a better career.

So what can be learned from reality? We should expect ups and downs and sideways and everything else in between. Expect to have several 2-3 year periods in you life when your career will not be rapidly improving. Learn to enjoy that time to develop non-work or hidden talents and enjoy life. Do not always worry about your career moving ahead rapidly because when the time is right it will.

Refocusing

When was the last time you focused on the little things in life? Can you remember the smell of a gardenia or the sound of an ocean? Have you recently experienced a cool summer morning with birds chirping? When was the last time you smelled fresh baking bread? Have you looked at the stars from a mountain side on a clear night? Have you walked through the leaves in the woods during fall? These little experiences can help you see the world and all of its beauty. Make a list of your ten most enjoyable activities. How many of these have you done lately? Try to do at least one per day.

Defining Success

Success, of course, can be defined in a multitude of ways, both on a large scale and in daily activities. Ask your friends about their successes and you will hear a wide variety of answers. If your career is not progressing the way you would like, there is no need to define success in a work related manner. In fact, for your happiness and mental health, look at other avenues of success. Individuals should seek non-career success inversely proportional to the amount of success they find in their work. In other words if you feel low career related success, seek a high degree of non-career related achievements. Conversely, if you have a great deal of success in your work, relax and enjoy your leisure time.

What is Success?

To laugh often and much:

To win the respect of intelligent
people and the affection of children;

To earn the appreciation of honest critics
and endure the betrayal of false friends;

To appreciate beauty;

To find the best in others;

To leave the world a bit better, whether by
a healthy child, a garden patch or a
redeemed social condition;

To know even one life has breathed easier
because you have lived;

This is to have succeeded.

—Ralph Waldo Emerson

Myths and Realities About Success

Myth 1: **The more money you have, the more successful you are.**

Reality: The more money you have, the more money you will need.

Myth 2: **Once you are successful, you can relax and enjoy life.**

Reality: Success is an ever changing goal.

Myth 3: **Monetary success will make you feel good about yourself.**

Reality: Many wealthy people receive psychotherapy.

Myth 4:   **Many people will look up to you if you make a great deal of money and impressive titles.**

Reality: You have to earn respect every day.

Myth 5:   **Success can be defined in material ways.**

Reality: Success is an internal feeling.

Money and Success: The First Mistake

"Money is not the measure of success" wrote Steven R. Covey, author of *The 7 Habits of Highly Successful People*. A reality is that money cannot buy a feeling of success. In fact necessity is often determined by income level. The more money you have the higher your necessities cost, therefore we get caught in a vicious cycle, and can never have enough. Success is an internal feeling and objects purchased do not give people a lasting feeling of success. How many possessions do you have now that at one time were emotionally uplifting? Count the number of art pieces, clothes and musical equipment or other possessions that once were exciting and now ignored. Are you considering other things to purchase to provide feelings of success? This habit is an expensive one and provides only temporary positive feelings.

A 1992 Roper poll for Shearson Lehman Brothers found that the median family income cited by 1,006 Americans as necessary to meet their wishes was $77,000. People with yearly incomes under $25,000 said $54,000 would be sufficient, while those earning $100,000 or more wanted $192,000. Individuals age 18-29 said they would need $80,000, while those 30-39 said $88,000 would be needed. Can Americans ever be financially and materially satisfied or will they always need more? It appears that "enough money" is an elusive goal.

What are the major drawbacks of monetary measures of success?. By using this measure, you will probably not have:

- Free time to enjoy life and its simple pleasures,
- A feeling of control over your life because you must always be seeking more,
- A feeling you have enough, unless you earn millions of dollars a year,
- A real sense of success because of high expectations, from yourself or significant others,

- A sense of accomplishment that comes from being concerned about helping others.

Careers and Success: The Second Mistake

In our society many people seek careers that they hope will make them feel successful and fulfilled. They assume career success will spill over into other areas of their life. Unfortunately this puts a great deal of pressure on a career to improve their entire lives and does not allow time for other areas of their personality to develop. According to Carol Gilligan, women have a more humanistic view of success which incorporates the goals of personal relationships with job achievements. Failure at home means failure in one's career and teamwork is placed above individual achievements.

Obviously, careers cannot provide success in other areas of our lives and time must be spent in those areas.

Personal Development First

Even though it is often ignored, life is a developmental process that goes on from birth to death. In order to attain success in your life, personal areas will need to be developed BEFORE YOU TRY TO IMPROVE YOUR CAREER. If this is not done, chances are good that you may fall back into the same unfulfilling work and lack of success as before. We cannot ignore basic personality issues and hope to find satisfying careers. Look at people who find employment easily or are the last to be laid off, and you will see many personal characteristics that are highly developed.

Success Paths

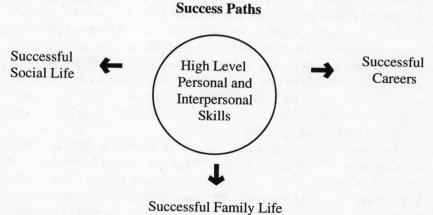

Successful Social Life ← High Level Personal and Interpersonal Skills → Successful Careers

↓

Successful Family Life

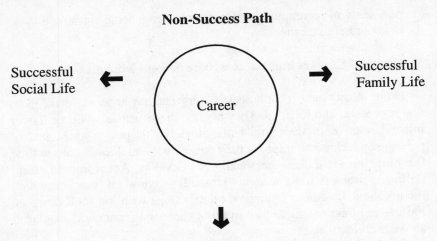

Non-Success Path

Successful Social Life ← Career → Successful Family Life

↓

High Level Interpersonal Skills

DEFINING OUR OWN SUCCESS

Each of us must develop OUR OWN criteria of what it takes to be successful. To do this, in itself, is an excellent indication of success because it means we are internally focused. Influence on personal success ideas comes from parents, family, work associates, neighbors and others. Often we marry individuals who have the exact same definition of success as our parents.

So how do you construct your own definition of success? First, describe yourself and your positive qualities without talking about your career. How many good characteristics can you list that are not career related, or can be used in non-career activities. For example you might say that you are warm, caring, a good father or mother, a quick learner, sensitive to people's feelings, in good health, etc. There are probably many successful and positive sides to yourself that are non-career related.

Think of a time in the past few years when you felt successful. What was it like? What were you doing? Were you helping a friend or child with a problem? Were you playing a sport? Were you painting or building something? What non-career skills were you using? Relax and enjoy that experience for a few minutes.

Give yourself some pats on the back for past accomplishments rather than ignoring or diminishing them. What did you do to achieve that success? What gave those particular experiences a feeling of success to you? Often feelings of success come from smaller achievements such as learning to play a song rather than larger ones such as getting a college degree. It is very important to review your successes and accomplishments over the past few years. Take an hour and complete the following exercise. On a blank sheet of paper write two or three accomplishments you personally feel good about that happened during the following time frames:

- Ten to eighteen years of age:
- Nineteen to twenty-five:
- Twenty-six to thirty-four:
- Thirty-five to forty-five:
- Forty-five to sixty:
- Over sixty:

Next to each accomplishment describe, what you were doing and what made it feel like an accomplishment.

Example

	Accomplishment	Why it felt good
Age 11 to 18	Was in senior play in high school	Helped me get over my fear of public speaking Recognition
	Played sports	Being part of a winning team
	Elected VP of high school class	Recognition, leadership
Age 19 to 25	Completed college	Gave me a sense of being educated
	Bought first car	Sense of independence
Age 26 to 34	Moved to California	Out on my own New state
	Married	Commitment

	First child	Creating some-one incredible
Age 35 to 45	First professional job	Gave me a feeling of being a professional
	First publication	Recognition

Now, try to decide how often they involved the following (using examples):

- Social Interactions (e.g. working with people, group activities)   3
- Reading, learning (e.g. making good grades in class, doing a class project, learning something new)   1
- Managing, developing or persuading (e.g. starting your own business, elected to an office, public speaking, recognition)   3
- Doing something creative (e.g. painting, playing a musical instrument)   0
- Building something (e.g. woodworking, crafts, sewing, car repairs)   0
- Getting things organized or straight (keeping your room neat, balancing your checkbook)   0

Next, prioritize your success in terms of how often they happened. For example:

- 1st—Managing, performing, persuading
- 2nd—Social activities
- 3rd—Learning
- 4th—Building something
- 5th—Artistic endeavors
- 6th—Keeping things neat and organized

This is the pattern you need to follow in order to feel successful for now. Later other areas may be at the top of your list. Life is a developmental process in which successful people deal with the most important issues first and wait to work on others as they emerge. Unsuccessful people often try to do everything at once.

There are many ways to fulfill success in each of the six areas described above. Some examples are:

- **Social**—Do volunteer work in a social service agency. Get to know your neighbors and help them in some way. Spend more time with children. Organize social events.

- **Artistic**—Work for a local arts council. Do photography or take arts classes. Volunteer at an art museum.

- **Mechanical**—Fix your car or mine. Help your neighbor repair something. Build something that can be sold at a fund raiser.

- **Leadership**—Organize a neighborhood activity dealing with a local problem. Participate in local politics or school programs.

- **Learning**—Take classes on subjects you would like learn more about. Read books and attend discussion groups. Attend seminars or workshops.

- **Organization**—Clean out closets or rooms in your house. Buy a home computer to keep records. Become treasurer of an organization.

It is important to start your success drive with small goals and build momentum. List one or two activities you would like to pursue in your top category. Also think about obstacles and ways to overcome them. Different levels of participation are available such as:

- **Learning Level**—to become more familiar with the activity.

- **Organizer**—to plan events and coordinate people and activities (e.g. organize the neighborhood charity fund raising campaign). This is a good way to improve your management skills.

- **Publicist**—by writing ads or designing posters.

- **Promoter**—by making phone calls or selling the ideas to others.

Additional Success Activities

Risk—Feelings of success can often come from participating in activities with some amount of risk. The excitement of doing something new and daring usually lifts our energy level, gives new confidence and expands our abilities. These activities do not have to be life threatening to give feelings of success. Some examples of risk taking behavior might be running for public office, public speaking, traveling somewhere new, joining a men's or women's support group, learning to sail, or going places to meet new people.

Identify three activities that intimidate you a little but would be good for your growth.

New Interests

Seeking success in areas that are the opposite of your everyday work can bring new energy into your work and provide a break from normal routine. Some examples are engineers who play musical instruments; carpenters who work with kids on simple building projects; social workers who do crafts for hobbies.

Group Success

Another way to feel better about yourself is to look beyond an individual definition of success towards group accomplishments. This group can be your family, city, state, neighborhood, or other group. You can focus on people, animals, plants or the entire earth. Try to think of two or three group accomplishments that you might pursue in the next few months.

Life Success Inventory

Most of us are satisfied with parts of our life and dissatisfied with other areas. Take the survey below to assess your growth directions. Circle the number to the right that best represents your degree of satisfaction with life. Give several examples in each area of how things are going well or need improvement. If you cannot find several pieces of supporting evidence, your assessment may be inaccurate.

| | Needs Improvement | | | Going Well |

1. Social Relationships/Family/Friendships
   (Evidence:_____
   _____)

       1   2   3   4   5

2. Communication Skills
   (Evidence:_____
   _____)

       1   2   3   4   5

3. Self Control
   (Evidence:_____
   _____)

       1   2   3   4   5

4. Exercise
   (Evidence:_____
   _____)

       1   2   3   4   5

5. Diet
   (Evidence:_____
   _____)

       1   2   3   4   5

6. Assertiveness
   (Evidence:_____
   _____)

       1   2   3   4   5

7. Creativity
   (Evidence:_____
   _____)

       1   2   3   4   5

8. Decision Making Abilty
   (Evidence:_____
   _____)

       1   2   3   4   5

9. Helping Others
   (Evidence:_____
   _____)

       1   2   3   4   5

10. Leisure Activities
    (Evidence:_____
    _____)

        1   2   3   4   5

11. Personal Growth
   (Evidence:_____
   _____)
                           1   2   3   4   5

12. Stress Relievers
   (Evidence:_____
   _____)
                           1   2   3   4   5

13. Financial Management
   (Evidence:_____
   _____)
                           1   2   3   4   5

14. Other Areas Not Mentioned
   (Evidence:_____
   _____)
                           1   2   3   4   5

ASSESSING YOUR SUCCESS QUOTIENT

Add the numbers you have circled to get your sum. If you scored between:

55-70	You probably are quite successful and are moving ahead with your life.
42-54	There is room for improvement in some areas.
30-41	There are several areas to improve upon
Below 30	Seek supportive counseling

Next look at the areas that are going well. How are you able to make these go well while other areas are less so? Review the areas you feel are less well developed and rated lower. Prioritize them in terms of most important to work on now. Remember you cannot work on everything at once and be successful. Later you will have time to work on other areas of your life. Select one area that will be enjoyable or relatively easy to improve. Write down your "now-growth" area on a sheet of paper and what ideally you would prefer it to be like. At the end of one month add a second area to improve.

Setting Up Your Success Committee

It should come as no surprise that career and personal issues can only be partially solved alone. Review how you have come this far in life and you will see that many people have helped and supported you along the way. They may not have said "I am going to help you" but rather did it in subtle ways. Everyone needs support and feedback. Set up an informal success committee to give you ideas, suggestions, and feedback on how you are doing. On your success committee you will need the following:

- One chairperson who is very skilled in the area you are trying to improve upon to tell you if you are on the right track,
- Two or three peers or co-workers who will help you move in the right direction,
- One or two supporters who will always tell you that you are doing a great job regardless of the truth,
- Two or three clients who will give you feedback on your quality of service and make suggestions for improvements.

Not everyone you ask will want to be on your committee and members may need to be added or deleted from time to time. Once you have your success committee in place it is time to informally call your first meeting, and solicit feedback, ideas and suggestions about your success goals and planned activities. It is best to meet individually or in small groups with your committee once or twice every month. Smaller groups make it less intimidating to you and gives a greater chance for rapport and input. What do you want to ask about or discuss with your committee?

- How you are feeling and why you would like more non-career success in your life.
- How you would like to be more successful.
- How you are going about improving your success.
- What you would like from them.

Allow them to give you ideas, suggestions and honest feedback.

Getting Started Today

Successful people have four things in common. First, they decide what to accomplish. Second they set goals and break them down into manageable components. Third, they start with an area that they are assured of success in order to "build up steam." And fourth they plunge ahead and "just do it." They are not afraid of failure and instead deal with obstacles as they arise. Let's try the same strategies for you on an activity that you would like to accomplish this next month.

One Significant Goal for the Next Month:

Activities Needed to Reach This Goal

1. _____
2. _____
3. _____

Which Activity Will Be Easiest to Start With and Accomplish?

- Potential barriers to achieving the first activity.
- Resources and methods to overcome these barriers.
- People who can help you attain these goals.

Discovering Your Natural Work Rhythms

Some people have the highest energy and creativity in the morning while others do best in the afternoon or evening. Success will come easier if you work during the period in which your energy level is highest. Energy level is often based upon what happened the previous day. Chart your energy level by putting a one (lowest) to five (highest) rating next to every hour of your waking day for the next week. The highest level may never be achieved (fives) so work should be done when your energy gets to a three or four. Take note of diet, drink, sleep, exercise and their relation to your personal energy.

Recommended Readings

Be Your Best. Linda Adams. Perigree Press, 1989.

Risking. David Viscott. Pocket Books, 1977.

Success Through a Positive Mental Attitude. Napoleon Hill. Pocket Books. 1987.

The Evolving Self. Mihaly Csikszentmihalyi. Harper, 1993.

The 7 Habits of Highly Successful People. Steven Covey Simon & Schuster, 1990.

The Psychology of Winning. Dennis Waitly. Berkeley Books, 1984.

4

RELATIONSHIPS & COMMUNICATIONS: MAJOR KEYS TO SUCCESS

*D*eveloping and improving relationships is one of the major keys to success in life.

Don was a college student in 1970 doing an internship with a local radio station. One of the station managers liked him and offered him a full time position upon graduation. Twenty years later, Don is a director of sports programs in a major U.S. market and makes over $300,000 a year. "Being liked" is one of the major ingredients in a successful life.

Regardless of the type of career style you select, having positive relationships with your supervisor, co-workers, friends, family members and acquaintances is extremely important. We all know people who had problems with relationships and their work was affected negatively. Job interviews are primarily an assessment of personality and social skills including friendliness, energy, enthusiasm, communication skills, honesty and decision making ability.

The most successful people in our society give and receive a great deal from relationships. Gloria, owner of a small clothing store, recently ran her first marathon race, at the age of forty-five. The first twenty miles were relatively easy but during the next two miles she began experiencing pain. At the twenty-two mile mark she considered stopping. Several of her friends saw her slowing down and ran along side, outside of the race track for a quarter mile while cheering. After ending the race, Gloria said that finishing the race would have been impossible without friends' support. Have you had these types of experiences? If so, you realize that we cannot grow, change and achieve without support from friends.

What are the characteristics of positive relationships?

- They are open and honest. You can tell people your secrets, wishes and concerns.
- They are supportive and caring. Helping each other during difficult times is the norm.
- Mutual interests are shared. You enjoy the same activities and share them often.
- They have flexibility. You relate in a variety of ways as a parent, adult and child.

How many positive relationships do you have? The healthy individual needs at least one positive relationship in every situation in which he/she spends more than four hours a week.

UNDERSTANDING DIFFERENCES IN HUMAN BEHAVIOR

Most people can be understood in terms of personality differences and similarities. John Holland, author of *Making Vocational Decisions* describes six different types of personalities.

- **Social Types** are very open and friendly, talk a lot, enjoy sharing their feelings, have many friends, like to attend parties and solve problems by discussing them with others.
- **Investigative Types** are analytical, like to work on computers, perform scientific activities, and solve problems in a methodical, analytical way.
- **Artistic Types** are creative, like to paint, play musical instruments and work in unstructured and non-pressured situations.
- **Realistic Types** like to work with their hands, fix and repair, and be in concrete situations.
- **Enterprising Types** like to manage and lead, be challenged, and solve problems on their own.

- **Conventional Types** like structure, being organized, having schedules and planning ahead.

Each of these types solve problems differently. For example when getting lost while driving in a new city, social types are most likely to stop and ask for directions. Investigative types will usually take out a map and try to find directions. Enterprising people will search for the location on their own. Conventional types rarely get lost because they have carefully mapped out the directions before leaving home. Artistic types usually enjoy getting lost and do not worry about being some place on time.

Can you tell among your friends, relatives, neighbors and co-workers who is which type? If not, try casually asking them the following questions.

What are their favorite hobbies?

- Realistic types like to build and repair.
- Artistic types like to read, go to movies and plays.

What they like and dislike about their work?

- Social types like the people.
- Enterprising types like the challenge.
- Artistic types like the freedom and creativity.

What accomplishments they felt good about during the past year?

- Social types like helping people.
- Realistic types like repairing.
- Enterprising types like recognition.

What they majored in during college?

- Conventional types majored in accounting.
- Investigative types majored in science or engineering.
- Artistic types majored in fine arts, film, music or theater.

Improving Relationships with These Types

Once you have discovered the typology of an individual it will be easier to relate to them.

- **Social types** like for you to be friendly, supportive and easy going. Ask social types about their family and suggest doing things together or invite them to your house.

- **Realistic types** do not like to talk a lot but rather prefer to let their work do the talking for them. It is no accident that most auto repair shops have a service manager to talk to you about your car. The actual repair person rarely talks to the customers because they usually do not feel comfortable relating to people. Spotting realistic types in your neighborhood is easy because they have a variety of tools in their garage and are often repairing or building around their house. Becoming friends with realistic types can save many hours of frustrating and unsuccessful repair work.

- Relating to people using facts and information is easiest for **investigative types.** Therefore when talking with an investigative person do not be put off by their knowledge of detail and facts. Ask investigative types facts about their area of expertise and you will have made a friend.

- **Artistic types** like to talk about music, plays, movies and other creative activities. It is best to talk with artistic types about these interests rather than their job.

- Whether you asked them or not, **enterprising types** like to tell you about their accomplishments. Better be ready to listen because enterprising people are much better talkers than listeners. Ask enterprising people their opinions and accomplishments.

- **Conventional types** are somewhat shy in social interactions, therefore you need to reach out to them. Ask them about their work and family. Religion is also very important to conventional types.

POSITIVE RELATIONSHIPS AT WORK

The major reason people get fired from their jobs is having poor relationships with their co-workers and/or supervisor, not inability to do the job. Poor relationships are caused by conflicts that are resolved with one winner and one loser rather than a win-win solution. Also, if we become too task and work oriented, little time is left for positive social interaction. On the other hand, being liked at work will provide more latitude to correct any problems that develop. How can you become more popular at work? Here are some hints.

- Ask co-workers about their weekends and vacations.
- Do not gossip, complain or whine.
- Say hello to everyone with whom you come in contact at work.
- Help others when they are overwhelmed or have problems
- Plan fun events such as parties or lunches.
- Laugh at others' jokes.
- Bring food treats into the office.
- Listen to others comments and reflect their feelings.
- Personally wish everyone a happy birthday.
- Help others improve their jobs and careers.
- Tell funny stories about yourself.
- Show an interest in others' work.
- Find out what people enjoy and talk with them about it.
- Ask co-workers how their family is doing.
- Try to work together with others on special committees.
- Give people compliments on work well done or their dress.

What are the benefits of positive work relationships?

- People will help you when you need assistance.
- You can turn to others for advice.
- You will enjoy your job more.
- You will have someone to talk with when you are having conflicts with others.
- You will get promoted quicker into management positions.

MANAGING YOUR BOSS

The quickest way to get ahead, or get fired is to have poor communication or conflicts with your supervisor. Unfortunately most of us were never taught how to deal with our supervisor and learn by trial and error. Many recent college graduates have problems in this area because they have had minimum supervision from teachers.

What can you do to get along well with your supervisors?

- Listen very carefully to what they have to say. Some supervisors will tell you very clearly what their expectations are while others will be more subtle. Nevertheless you must play close attention to their requests and act on them quickly.

- Compliment your supervisor. Often we forget that supervisors need positive strokes also and may not be getting them from their bosses. Supervisors receive mostly complaints and problems. If you see something done well by your supervisor, let him or her know.

- Do not criticize your supervisor unless he or she asks for it. Even when it is asked for, criticize gently. Also remind him or her how well the "big picture" is going.

- Ask your supervisor about their interests or hobbies. Try to stay away from sensitive issues.

- Give your supervisor the limelight in newsletters, meetings or social events.

- Volunteer to help your supervisor on projects and go the extra steps to make his/her work easier.

- Develop special skills that your supervisor needs but does not want to personally acquire.

- Try to get along very, very well with your supervisor's personal assistant. This individual can make or break your career.

Personality Typology and Your Supervisor

Your supervisor's personality uniqueness, and your awareness of it can play a major role in mutual positive interactions.

- **Social Supervisors** place an emphasis on people getting along well in the office. They usually dislike conflict and prefer harmony over achievement. Be ready for a lot of meetings and discussions with this type of manager.

- **Enterprising Supervisors** prefer employees who develop new projects and find ways to bring more money or influence into the department. They are never quite satisfied and prefer achievement over harmony.

- **Conventional Supervisors** like an office that is well run, highly organized, with policies, procedures and time lines. Conventional supervisors develop forms for everything.

- **Artistic Managers** prefer an unstructured work environment, casual clothes, few policies and creative problem solving. New ideas and programs are encouraged.

- **Investigative Managers** prefer to research all the options before making any decisions, working at a slower pace, an informal work environment, and in-depth answers to issues.

Which type of manager do you prefer and have you been? Take a look at your previous supervisors with whom you related well. Which personality characteristic(s) most closely resemble them?

Things Your Boss Wants You to Know But Will Not Tell You

1. Understand your supervisor's language. "I don't want to rush you". . .means hurry. "If it is not too much trouble". . .means do it and the sooner the better.
2. Learn the big picture and what others are doing.
3. Learn to handle problems yourself.
4. Complain only when it is very important; do not be a whiner.
5. Always do a bit more than expected.
6. Take the initiate and be looking for things to do to improve the organization.
7. Complete the work, don't make excuses.
8. Anticipate problems and potential solutions.
9. Be discreet about people and organizational problems.
10. Learn to be punctual.
11. Take sick days when you are truly ill.
12. High quality, rather than perfection, will do.
13. Choose your battles carefully.

14. Learn to get along with co-workers because conflicts undermine productivity.
15. Read professional publications and stay up with what is going on in the field.
16. Develop a sense of timing, particularly when the boss does and does not want to talk.
17. Do not lie; you will lose your credibility.

Relationships With People You Supervise

The individuals you supervise are your most important clients. Unfortunately some supervisors see their staff as slaves. This type of supervision is being replaced in the U.S. with one that has the manager as consultant and resource. Supervising your staff include many of the same ways that we should relate to clients and our children.

- Give them the resources they need to succeed. This includes computer equipment, consultants, money, and assistance wherever necessary.

- Give the necessary training to do the work. The better trained they are, the higher quality of work.

- Present a lot of positive feedback. This feedback costs nothing and can be an extremely effective motivator. Even when people do not do well, let them know their efforts were noticed.

- Provide as much freedom as asked for at work. New employees usually need directions. Once the work is learned, the best way to keep them challenged is to give them the flexibility to mold the work to their personality, while still accomplishing office goals.

- Publicly recognize their accomplishments.

- Promote their professional growth. Some employees are working on undergraduate or graduate degrees. Others are involved in professional associations. Support and encourage your employees and they will work much harder.

Varying Your Relationship Style

No one likes a supervisor who is constantly telling employees what to do. Therefore, to have a good relationship with your staff, interact on several levels. At the PARENT level, you can tell them how they need to improve their work. At the ADULT level, talk about the current work situation in a factual and realistic way, with give and take. Let them make suggestions for improvement of services and operations. On the CHILD level, joke around and have fun together. By relating on all three levels an individual will become more comfortable with you, be open and honest, respect you, and likely listen more to your suggestions.

Relationships With Persons Above Your Supervisor

Having a friendly relationship with your bosses' supervisor is good politics. This individual can help with your career development and come to your assistance if trouble develops with your direct supervisor. Be careful not to criticize your supervisor to his/her superiors.

- Say hello to your boss' supervisor whenever you can.
- Talk to him or her at company functions.
- Ask about his or her interests.
- Compliment him/her on something he/she did.
- Ask him/her to write something for your publication, and give him/her an outline.
- Help his/her friends, children or assistants whenever possible.

Needless to say, it is not enough to do high quality work to be successful. You must also put time and effort into social relationships. Although there is no specific formula, successful people spend at least one-fourth of work time developing and maintaining positive relationships.

Relationships With Clients

Personal service is the major reason clients use your organization. Small organizations without large advertising budgets particularly rely on word of mouth for new clients. Unless your product is the only one available in the world, the service you provide should be outstanding. Solicit feedback whenever possible from clients about your products and services.

Evaluating Your Work Relationships

How do you think your work relationships could improve? Of the areas described above, how would you rate them. Ask others, if you are not sure, or want more feedback.

Person	Rating (Good, Fair, Needs Work)	Potential Improvements
Co-workers		
Supervisor		
People above supervisor		
People you supervise		
Clients		

What to Do When Relationships Don't Work

Occasionally, our relationships at work deteriorate. This may be caused by competition for resources, lack of understanding, differences in personality or power needs. Often we are not even aware of what caused the problem. There are several ways to deal with the issues and conflicts.

- If the conflict is with your supervisor and you have a good relationship, the best advice is to talk directly about the conflict. It is important to understand the conflict and come to a amiable solution. Without knowing the causes, you have no way to correct it. Most supervisors will respect you for bringing up and dealing with conflicts in an effort to resolve them.

- Conflicts with co-workers can waste a lot of time. Ignoring the problem might work if both of you are not together very often. If your work interaction is frequent it is best to deal with the conflict directly, in a non-blaming style. Let the other individual know that you would like to improve your work relationship. Try to be specific and positive about each other's contributions but do not avoid the issues. See if you can work out a solution that is satisfactory by getting together periodically to discuss progress. Most people prefer compromise over conflict.

Word will spread in your office if you have conflicts with your staff, primarily from them to their friends. Therefore it is very important to deal with the conflict in a positive way. First of all, talk directly about the conflict and why it bothers you. A staff member may have little or no idea that the problem exists. Second, try to understand what is causing the problem. Is it lack of skills, time, information or experience? Allow your staff to develop potential solutions to the conflict. Discuss the options and agree on a solution. Schedule follow up meetings for assessment or look at other options.

Positive Relationships Outside of Work

We all need individuals to help us develop and maintain our life. The easiest way to do this is by setting up your "Relationship Cabinet." This cabinet will include membership of people in a variety of areas of which you can benefit from their skills. Most of us need six to twelve cabinet advisors. They might include any of the following:

Secretary of Fun or Travel
Secretary of Finances
Secretary of Home Repair
Secretary of Social Relationships
Secretary of Creativity
Secretary of Health
Secretary of Spirituality
Secretary of Decision Making
Secretary of Quality Control
Secretary of Risk Taking
Secretary of Work/Career Development

First, identify at least four areas of your life in which support is needed for personal growth. Second, find one or two people who, just by their natural ability, can help you develop in these areas. Third, spend quality time with them at least once a month.

Recommended Reading

Contemporary Business Communication. Scott Ober. Houghton Mifflin, 1992.

Making Vocational Choices. John L. Holland. Prentice Hall, 1985.

The Gentle Art of Verbal Self Defense. Suzette Elgin. Prentice Hall, 1980.

Type Talk at Work. Otto Kroeger and Janet Thuesen. Delta Books, 1992.

Working at Human Relations. Rosemary Fruehling. McGraw Hill, 1977.

You Can Negotiate Anything. Herb Cohen. Bantam Books, 1988.

You Just Don't Understand Me: Women and Men in Conversation. Deborah Tannen. Ballentine Books, 1991.

5 | PERSONAL GROWTH & SUCCESS

*I*magine yourself strolling through the woods on a clear and warm summer day. As you meander, you pick up three or four things. These can be natural such as flowers and wood or man-made objects such as paper or clothing. After gathering these objects you decide to toss away all of them except one. What is this object, why did you keep it and what significance does it have in your life?

A colleague recently participated in this exercise and surprisingly picked up a cigarette lighter in his fantasy walk. He realized that this fantasy was telling him more spark and fire was needed in his life. What do you need in your life?

SELF DISCIPLINE

In his best selling book, *The Road Less Traveled*, Scott Peck states that "discipline is the basic set of tools required to solve life's problems. Without discipline we can solve nothing." Self discipline is one of the major steering mechanisms that keeps us on track in our immediate gratification society and without it we meander into pitfalls. What areas of your life would you like to have greater control over? Eating, drinking, exercise and spending money are areas in which many Americans lack self discipline.

Self Discipline and Diet

"Control your diet and you control your life," a friend once said to me. In our food rich, microwave, drive-in restaurant society, this is easier said than done. Nowhere else in the world can human beings have instant access to such harmful foods as in the U.S. As evidence of this, we are the only society in the history of the world with a weight problem. Unfortunately, what frequently tastes best is the worst. At a buffet luncheon meeting last year a colleague placed an apple next to a tray of fudge brownies. At the end of the meeting, all brownies were taken but the apple remained. Someone should create an apple that tastes like brownies.

How To Increase Control Over Your Diet

1. Decide what you should decrease or eliminate.
2. Do not buy it.
3. Purchase a healthy substitute food and change it every two weeks.
4. Drink a lot of water.
5. Reward yourself with $1 every time you eat a healthy substitute food and not the bad one.
6. Stay away from people with unhealthy diets.
7. Tell people about your new diet plan.
8. Exercise frequently.

What would you like to eliminate from your diet?

Self Discipline and Exercise

The most difficult thing about exercise is getting started. Someone should develop a service of calling and asking clients if they have exercised today. If you have not, they will come over, help you put on your jogging or walking shoes, and gently escort you outside. Once we get going, the exercise is not bad and the resulting feeling is wonderful. Exercise is like anything else, the more you do it, the sooner a habit develops. Try to determine three or four times a week that exercise fits your schedule and stick to it, with only minor modifications. Find an exercise that is either very enjoyable (e.g. tennis) or convenient (e.g. jogging). Purchase expensive equipment for these activities so you will feel guilty if you do not do it. Decide if you would like to do it alone, with others, competitively or a combination of the above. If you get bored or tired of it, try some other form of exercise. Build exercise into your program and make it a habit.

Exercise Goals for This Week

1. _____
2. _____
3. _____

ASSERTIVENESS

How often have you wished that you had spoken out in a discussion but remained quiet. Have you ever wondered about the bill at a restaurant or store but figured it was not worth bringing up. Ever been to a social gathering in which you wanted to meet someone but could not muster up the courage and missed an opportunity to make a friend? All of these are examples of success opportunities that were missed. Americans are assertive only 50-60 percent of the time they should be. Businesses understand this and overcharge us millions each year.

Why do we remain silent or without action when assertiveness can make us feel better and more successful?

- Fear of being wrong.
- Thinking that your needs are not as important as others.
- Not wanting to hurt another's feeling.
- Not being sure your idea is good enough.
- Fear of rejection, whether it be an idea or from a person.

Being Pleasantly Assertive

Often people are quiet and hope things work out. When that does not happen they become frustrated and aggressive. Finding that middle ground, where you are assertive but nice at the same time, is the key. Several elements are involved in being pleasantly assertive.

- First, know what you really want.
- Second, know where to obtain it.
- Third, smile, be upbeat and friendly.
- Fourth, lean forward and look the person in the eye.

- Fifth, tell them exactly what you need but in a very nice tone, not demanding.
- Sixth, repeat it so they know how important it really is.
- Seventh, do not leave until you receive a satisfactory answer or response.

Learning Assertive Behavior

Putting Yourself Down

Often we start our sentences with non-assertive phrases that should be eliminated.

- "I hate to bother you. . ."
- "When you have a minute. . ."
- "This is a dumb question. . ."
- "You may think that this is stupid. . ."
- "I know I shouldn't ask. . ."

Instead, begin your sentences with:

- "I have a great idea. . ."
- "This information will be very helpful to you. . ."
- "I recently read that. . ."

Voice Tone And Body Language

Voice tone and body language can be indications that you are not an assertive person. Practice standing tall and looking the person in the eye. Try to get as close as possible, particularly if you are trying to be very assertive.

Greeting People

One major element of successful communications is being able to greet strangers easily in safe situations. To increase comfort in greeting strangers, talk positively about a common experience or object that is close by; for example, "That is a pretty flower, what kind do you think it is?" "What a beautiful morning." Conversation seems to flow from that point, particularly if you look the person in the eye and smile. If the person does not want to talk, just move on and find someone else.

Giving and Accepting Compliments

Successful people constantly give and accept genuine compliments. Compliments are the "perfume of relationships." They can be very small (e.g. an article of clothing) or large (e.g. you have beautiful children) but must be sincere. Think about the compliments you remember and what made them memorable. Usually these are given in situations where we are less self assured therefore they build confidence. Therefore if you can find a person who is new to a situation and compliment them on something they are trying hard to do, you will have made a friend.

Asking For Clarification and Requesting Help

All of us have questions several times during the week. Unsuccessful people "fake it" and successful people ask for clarification and assistance. It is a lot worse to make mistakes due to lack of information than ask for help.

Speaking Up

Is it somewhat intimidating to speak at a meeting or in a group? If so, try doing it gradually. First tell someone that they have a good idea. Second, ask for clarification on a point. Third, make a suggestion. Fourth, disagree with someone that you honestly find differences with. These gradual steps can make it easier to talk, particularly in a new group.

Rehearsing Your Assertiveness

It is important when you first start down the path of assertiveness to know exactly what you want to say. Later, it will become more natural, easier and more spontaneous. There are several components of assertive statements which include

1. The behavior or situation that irritates you.
2. How the situation makes you feel.
3. What you would like to happen.
4. What the benefits of change are for everyone.

An Example:

"Your dog barks throughout the night and keeps me awake. This really annoys me and causes me to lose a great deal of sleep. Please keep your dog inside at night. If you do this I won't have to call the animal control warden or you in the middle of the night."

Always try to be nice but firm when being assertive. If you are nasty, people will reject your request just because they do not like you. The intensity level can always be increased.

During the next week, be assertive by:

1. Making small talk with a stranger.
2. Giving three compliments to people you know.
3. Asking for clarification.
4. Disagreeing with someone at work

THE 2 + 1 + 1 RULE

Often, individuals will ask us to do things that we prefer not to, but we accept because of not knowing how to say no. The 2 + 1 + 1 rule is a sophisticated way to deny requests without offending others.

First, give two statements that acknowledge you have heard the individuals request. Second, tell them why you cannot agree. Third, give them a good option.

For example, a person wants you to help them with a project that is due in two days. You might say:

"I understand how important this project is to you and how much pressure you feel to complete it. I cannot help you now because I have been planning my vacation for two months and have already paid 50% of it. Can you ask Sue's assistant, Mark? He is having a work lull this week."

Another example is a social gathering you have been asked to attend by a friend.

"Thank you for inviting me, I know it will be a fun event and that you would like to have companionship. Unfortunately, I already have plans. Would you like to have lunch later in the week."

This technique recognizes an individual's needs and request, and lets that individual know you are trying to help solve the problem.

STRESS REDUCTION

Most people have a great deal of stress in their lives at certain times, a moderate amount at other times and low amounts infrequently. In our complex and fast-paced society, it would be nearly impossible to be stress free for long periods of time. Regardless, it is healthy to try to control stress but unrealistic to eliminate it forever. Think about some of the most stressful days or weeks you have had in the last year and the probable causes. Was there anything you could have done to avoid the stress and how you dealt with it? Was the stress something that you caused (e.g. taking on a great deal more responsibility at work), or something beyond your control (e.g. traffic accident that made you late for a meeting)? What have you learned from these experiences? If the answer is "nothing," they most surely will be repeated again.

Dealing With Stress

Assuming that there will be stress in our lives, what can we do about it? Some suggestions include:

- Adopt an attitude of "that's life."
- Exercise for thirty minutes at least four times a week.
- Listen to relaxing music.
- Go to more movies, plays and concerts.
- Take more short vacations.
- Drink less caffeinated coffee.
- Get more sleep or sleep better by relaxing one hour before bed time, drinking warm milk, taking a hot shower or bath, and keeping the bedroom temperature between 68 and 75 degrees.
- Resolve ongoing conflicts.
- Stop over-committing yourself.
- Take long baths.
- Get a massage.
- Play more, do something silly or child-like for a change.
- Face problems with a positive attitude.

Three Stress Reducers You Will Use This Week

1. _____
2. _____
3. _____

Dealing with Your Fears

A client of mine, Michael, was going to be interviewing with an organization the following week for a position that he highly coveted. Michael had attended an interview workshop but still felt there might be other ways to prepare. When I suggested that he do a video practice interview, he thought about it for a minute and said, "that feels really scary. If it scares me that much I should do it." This attitude is best for fostering our personal growth. Hiding from our fears stops our development, while confronting and overcoming them will provide energy for personal growth. Anything you are unwilling to experience runs your life.

What are some common fears among Americans?

- Fear of heights
- Fear of flying
- Fear of public speaking
- Fear of rejection
- Fear of failure
- Claustrophobia

Do any of these fears seem familiar to you? Think of two or three fears that you would like to get rid of.

1. _____
2. _____
3. _____

Karen, an attractive female aged 27, was very shy and had a fear of meeting new people. While most people her age were having fun, Karen rented movies frequently. Along with the movies came junk food and 22 extra pounds. After getting extremely bored, Karen decided to take a four week class on meeting people. She made two new friends in the class and ended up going to many new social events. Within the next month, Karen lost twelve pounds and felt a great deal better about herself.

Fears can hold us back from progressing in our work. Carol, a forty year old woman grew up in the pre-computer age and had a fear of them. When told by her supervisor that her work was lacking because she wasn't using the information available on her computer, she started crying. With support from other staff members, Carol learned the basics and found computer usage not as difficult as she imagined. Later, she took several computer classes and became more comfortable with using the machines. The feeling of success and energy released from overcoming her fear made Carol's work evaluation the best one in several years.

There are several ways to get rid of your fears. These include:

- Reading books such as the ones listed at the end of this chapter.
- Learning real facts related to unrealistic fears.
- Taking a class or workshop.
- Talking to a professional psychologist or counselor.
- Dealing directly with the problem and talking to others about it.
- Coming up with your own creative solutions.

Try not to overwhelm yourself and attempt to change several behaviors at once. Review all of the change you would like to make and prioritize them. Rank them in terms of difficulty. Start with the easier ones first to build up steam before tackling more difficult ones. If you are having difficulty with the more challenging behaviors; take courses, read books and talk with professionals.

Additional Resources

Conquering Stress. KRS Ed Strom. Barrons Books, 1993.

Feel the Fear and Do it Anyway. Susan Jeffers. Fawcett Columbine, 1987.

Speaking up. Mark Ruskin. Bob Adams Books, 1993.

Stress Without Distress. Hans Selye. Signet, 1974.

The Anxiety and Phobia Workbook. Edmund J. Bourne. New Harbinger Press, 1990.

When I Say No, I Feel Guilty. Manuel J. Smith. Bantam Books, 1975.

You Don't Have to Take it. Ginny Nicarthy, Naomi Gottlieb, Sandra Hoffman. Seal Press, 1993.

Your Phobia. Manuel Zane and Harry Milt. Warner Books, 1984.

The Road Less Traveled. M. Scott Peck. Simon & Schuster, 1978.

6

TOUCHING YOUR CREATIVE SIDE & DEVELOPING YOUR DECISION MAKING SKILLS

*S*uccessful individuals are often able to call upon both their creative and logical sides. They know an imbalance toward one side can cause frustration and incompleteness. For example, vacations that are too planned with little opportunity for spontaneity tend to feel confining. On the other hand trips that are disorganized get frustrating. Finding a creative and logical balance will help your life journey be more successful.

DEVELOPING CREATIVITY

Creativity is a natural talent for some individuals, while most of us have to develop it. Creativity is not only defined as the ability to play a musical instrument or paint, but also the capacity to think abstractly and develop new ideas. Ways to develop creativity include being around creative people, taking more vacations, attending seminars on topics unrelated or related to your work, listening to music, going to ethnic restaurants, sitting by the ocean, being in the mountains, watching science fiction movies and reading. Let's do some exercises to develop creativity. Ask yourself the following questions:

- How many different ways can a spoon be used?
- What names would you give your plants?
- If down feathers are so warm, why do geese fly south for the winter?
- If you were to start a company, what would you name it and what would be its products and services?
- If you won the state lottery and had one million dollars a year to spend, how would you do it?
- What would your city look like if you could redesign it?
- If you had the power to change one or two major events in history, what would you change?
- What would you do to change our society in the next twenty years?
- What invention should be developed to make your life easier?
- Answer "who are you" in at least five different ways.
- Choose a single symbol, picture or other graphic which you feel best represents you, your work, your life.
- Write a four word headline about yourself, based upon your life.
- Imagine yourself as a salesperson who is selling_____.
- A sports star who is playing_____.
- An artist who paints _____.
- An author who is writing a book about_____.
- A builder who is constructing_____.
- A musician who plays_____.

Are you a:

- young Turk or wise old Greek?
- alley cat or house pet?
- meandering creek or rippling lake?
- sharply hit grounder or towering fly ball?
- strong bull or a quick bunny?

What would you do if you were a:

- public relations manager of a rat laboratory?
- designer of dumpsters?
- creative writer of IRS tax forms?
- acquisitions manager of an alligator swamp?
- time and motion study analyst of chicken plucking factory?
- proposal reviewer for agency that has no funds?

Try to think creatively with your daily problems, by developing three or four potential solutions before deciding on one.

Unscheduled Creativity

Creativity usually comes when we least expect it, often presenting itself while you are exercising, showering, before going to sleep or at meetings. Welcome creativity at any time and it will appear more often. Shut it off and it gets offended and leaves. How can you welcome creativity? Write down what it has to say immediately. Carry a creativity note pad wherever you go and collect ideas. You may be surprised how often it returns if you recognize and honor it.

Now look at several issues you are trying to resolve in your life. These might include selecting a career direction, resolving a conflict with a neighbor or dealing with overweight problems. Think of three or four creative ways to deal with these issues and write them on a piece of paper.

DECISION MAKING

We use a variety of decision making methods everyday. Some methods are more effective and work better depending upon the situation. Examples of decision making styles include:

- **Impulsive:** Little thought or examination, taking the first alternative, "leap before your look."

- **Delaying:** Taking a moratorium, postponing thought and action, "cross that bridge later."

- **Fatalistic:** Letting the environment decide, leaving it up to fate, "it's all in the cards."

- **Agonizing:** Getting lost in all the data, getting overwhelmed with analyzing alternatives, "I don't know what to do."

- **Compliant:** Let someone else decide, follow someone else's plans, "anything you say."

- **Paralysis**: The decision maker accepts responsibility but is unable to approach it, "I can't face up to it."

- **Intuitive:** Having an unconscious sense of knowing, "it feels right."

We have used all of these styles at one time or another. If one is used too often, poor decisions or indecisiveness may result. For decisions with minor consequences (e.g. what shoes to wear to work) just about any of the above methods except delaying and agonizing will work. For major decisions like which house or car to purchase, a more in-depth approach is best. What are the steps in a quality decision making process?

1. **Self Assessment:** Decide first what is most important to you. For example, if you are buying a house, rate the factors below as most, moderate, and least important to you:

    1. Cost,
    2. Neighborhood,
    3. Location of schools,
    4. Closeness to shopping,
    5. Nearby bus routes,
    6. Resale history,
    7. Quietness,
    8. Age of home,
    9. Condition of home,
    10. Landscaping,
    11. Upkeep,
    12. Number of rooms,
    13. Size of rooms,
    14. Layout of house, etc. . .

    Review a major decision you are facing and all of the factors to consider. Next, rate them as most important, moderate and least important.

2. **Exploration:** During this step, gather as much information as possible concerning the factors deemed important. For example, visit and preview as many houses as possible. Explore neighborhoods even though there are no listings. Talk with people about their areas of town and read information from real estate listings.

3. **Experience:** In this step, trying out the options gives concrete

experience on how it feels. For example, it would be wonderful if we could spend a week in a house before deciding to purchase it. This is difficult, so what is the next best strategy? Spend as much time as possible exploring the neighborhood at different times, talking with neighbors, examining the house, and bringing in inspectors or friends with similar values.

4. **Decide:** At this point a decision will be made. The perfect answer may not exist, therefore you will need to compromise on some things that are less important or wait until a later time, if possible. The decision making grid below can help weigh options.

First, list the most important factors across the top from most important to least important. Second, list all the homes in your final list that are appealing. Third, put excellent, good, fair, poor in the intersecting spaces. For example,

	Factors			
	Landscaping	Close to Parks	Quietness	Nice Neighbors
House A	poor	good	fair	good
House B	excellent	good	good	good
House C	good	fair	good	good
House D	good	excellent	good	good

As you can see from this grid, houses B and D are equally appealing. Review the second most important set of factors for house D and B to see if that helps clarify the decision. If both are still tied, it probably will not make much difference which house you purchase and one may have been sold by now anyway.

5. **Implementation:** After the decision has been made, take steps to implement it. If uncertainty still exists talk with people for support. Large decisions, such as buying a house, are usually frightening, so understand and accept this fear. Also, remember that most decisions can be changed later.

Try using this decision making strategy with smaller decisions until it becomes comfortable. Before going clothes shopping, decide on colors, styles, prices, quality, present wardrobe needs, etc. . . Then follow the other steps described above and see if the decisions are easier. Compare these decisions to purchases made in the past year.

Hard Work

Lets face it, nothing significant can be accomplished without hard work. Your creative side can help you come up with ideas, decision making can help you with directions, but it takes hard work to complete goals. Some suggestions to get the work going include:

- Do the easiest part first to get moving.
- Take things in small segments or 30-60 minute time frames to feel success.
- Make a list of what needs to be done and check off each accomplishment.
- Pace yourself so you do not get burned out quickly.
- Reward yourself for each accomplishment.

REWARDING YOURSELF

Rewarding oneself is an art most of us need to improve upon. We reward ourselves and seek rewards from others in very peculiar ways. Notice how you reward yourself now for an accomplishment at work, for completing a task around the house, or helping someone with a problem. Do you just go on to another task or stop and say "good job?" Do you tell other people about your accomplishment or keep it to yourself? Do you negate the accomplishment and say anyone could have done it? If you feel guilty giving yourself a reward, your parents probably felt the same.

How often do you reward yourself; once a month or yearly? What did you do in the last few days that was an accomplishment and how did you reward yourself? Remind yourself at the close of each day about accomplishments and give yourself a reward for these.

Deciding on a Reward

The first step in developing a good reward program is to decide upon an enjoyable reward. Would you like a new article of clothing or a CD? How about a vacation to a new and beautiful place? Would you prefer to just have time to rest and relax? How would you REALLY like to be rewarded? Sometimes we cannot afford a big reward so smaller ones must do. Ice cream, movies, reading, a walk around the park are rewards within everyone's reach. Determine four or five small rewards that are personally satisfying.

Deciding How Often to Reward Yourself

Accomplishments are the stepping stones to major success so you should reward yourself for each accomplishment. If having your children make better grades makes you feel successful, then reward yourself and them for every hour you spend together on school work. If having a nice garden is your goal, reward yourself for planting seeds or pulling weeds. Be sure to reward yourself for time and work, not just outcomes. Keep a chart of your accomplishments. Reviewing these is an important reward in itself.

How to Pay for the Reward

Paying for rewards can be accomplished by eliminating wasteful daily purchases. It is very easy to spend $4-5 a day on things not needed. Why do we buy these unneeded items? We are subconsciously rewarding ourselves without really recognizing the need for rewards. The more we reward ourselves intentionally the less we will do it randomly. This may not be as much fun as impulsive rewards but self controlled rewards will help achieve more important goals.

Getting Other People to Reward You

Accomplishments and successes should be shared with others. The compliments received will provide additional motivation. People often shy away from talking about themselves and therefore lose out on an important source of rewards. Tell at least one person a day what you accomplished and ask them to do the same. If all your tasks in a day were failures, compliment others and your day will have been successful.

Additional Resources

Brain Building. Marilyn vos Savant and Lenore Fleischer. Bantam Books, 1990.

Career Decision Making and Planning. David W. Winefordner. McKnight, 1980.

Conceptual Blockbusting. John Adams. W.H. Freeman, 1974.

Creativity: The Magic Synthesis. Silvano Arieti. Basic Books, 1976.

Deciding: A Leader's Guide. H.B. Gelatt, Barbara Varenhorst, and Richard Carey. College Entrance Examination Board, 1972.

Drawing on the Right Side of the Brain. Betty Edwards. Tarcher Perigree Books, 1989.

Flow. Mihaly Csikszentmihalyi. Harper Collins, 1990.

The Creativity Question. Albert Rothenberg and Carl Hausman. Duke University Press, 1976.

The Creative Journal. Lucia Cappacchione. New Castle Publishing, 1989.

The Structure of Magic. Richard Bandler and John Grinder. Science and Behavior Books, 1976.

Use Both Sides of Your Brain. Tony Bozan. Plume Books, 1991.

7

LEISURE & LEARNING: THE ENJOYABLE ROADS TO SUCCESS

When was the last time you relaxed sitting by a stream or taking a walk in the woods? How long has it been since you walked along a beach or lay in the grass watching the clouds. Americans are losing their ability to relax. Often people who appear to be participating in leisure activities are not really relaxing. Take golf and tennis. Millions of Americans have taken up these games in the last ten years, to relax. Yet when you look at their faces and listen to their words, frustration and disappointment appear. Pleasurable outcomes that are fantasized usually do not come. These activities are not really relaxing but rather another form of work. Americans have a tendency to make their work play and their play work. Do you do this with any of your activities?

Enjoying Your Leisure

Leisure Attitudes

Socrates said, "Leisure is the best of all possessions." Disraeli once commented, "Increased means and increased leisure are the two civilizers of man." Bertrand Russel said, "To be able to fill leisure time intelligently is the last product of civilization."

Truly enjoying your leisure is very important but often not easy. If relaxation is not the outcome of the majority of your leisure activities, either find a way to enjoy the activity or take up another one. There are many ways to enjoy your leisure.

- Participate in activities where no score is kept, or do it without keeping score. Bike riding, reading and movies are good examples to follow. Golf, tennis and bowling are usually satisfying only if your scores are good or improving.

- Have some activities that you can do lazily and enjoy. John likes to see how slow he can ride his bike without it falling over. One day while riding in a popular local park he encountered a policeman who was keeping track of speeds to ensure that bikers did not exceed 15 MPH. When John passed the policeman, he was told that the needle on the speed gun did not even move. At that point John knew he had achieved his goal of zero miles per hour.

- Participate in leisure activities with friends, particularly ones who are easy going. If your bridge bowling or tennis group is too competitive, join or start another one.

- Change the rules to have more fun. Have you ever played cross country golf? Start in the bathroom of a house near a golf course and work your way downstairs out the front door. When you reach the golf course decide on a final destination without using the regular holes. The first person to reach the sand trap on the seventh green wins. Another game to play with golf is to give an award to the person with the fewest putts, sand shots, lost balls, three iron shots, etc.

How Much Leisure Should You Have?

In our busy and work oriented society, leisure is often equated with laziness, yet people have different leisure needs in their lives. Two or three hours of leisure a day is required by some individuals while others need only that same amount in a week. In general, the amount of leisure needed is related to what you grew up with and the amount of stress in your life. Did your parents enjoy and participate in leisure activities a great deal, either with or without their children? If so chances are good that leisure is part of your nature. If your regular work week is fairly easy for you, your leisure may be built into your lifestyle and not much more is needed. On the other hand if you feel a great deal of stress, it may be necessary to have 1-3 hours of leisure a day. People under high stress will often get sick when they could have avoided this illness with more leisure. Keep a record of your leisure time and stress level each week to determine the right balance for you.

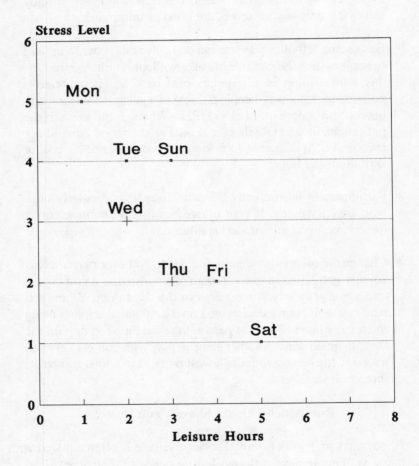

Timing of Leisure

The problem with retirement is that it comes so late in life that many activities cannot be enjoyed. A friend once suggested that we should retire in our twenties and thirties and work in later years. The same is true for timing of leisure. Often people participate in leisure at the end of the day or weekend, when they are very tired. Leisure activities are not as rewarding if we are too tired to enjoy them. Although every day cannot begin with hours of leisure, some days can. Try varying leisure time so that it occurs at different times of the day; some in the morning, afternoon and evening. If you wake up one day and feel that leisure is desperately needed, act on your instincts. You will enjoy that leisure a great deal more than putting it off until later.

SELECTING LEISURE ACTIVITY

Thousands of leisure activities are available to us. How can you possibly select the one that is most enjoyable to you? The steps involved are similar to those in selecting a career.

First do some needs assessment. Take the short questionnaire below and answer as you feel today.

1. How much physical activity would you like?

    _____a great deal _____moderate amount _____none

2. Would you prefer to be located—

    _____indoors _____outdoors _____ either

3. Would you prefer to be with people?

    _____a great deal _____somewhat _____not at all

4. Would you like the activity to last—

    _____one hour or less _____2-3 hours _____4 or more hours

5. What would you be willing to pay?

    _____less than $5 _____$5-10 _____$10-20
    _____$20-40 _____over $40

6. What skills would you like to use?

    _____intellectual _____physical _____creative _____manual

Once you have answered all of these questions, your personal leisure needs will be clarified. You may have to further prioritize these needs as:

- Most important—
- Secondary importance—
- Can live without—

Second, you should gather information on options for leisure. Thousands of options exist and can be grouped into the following categories.

Inexpensive Leisure Activities

camping   beachcombing
bicycling   movie watching
fishing   walking
kite flying   yoga

Social Activities

bridge   bowling
backgammon   doubles tennis
dancing   tutoring
sports watching   charades
auction attending   shopping
cooking clubs   refereeing

Pet Related Activities

aquarium owner   bird owner
zoo watcher   animal trainer
animal breeder

Intellectual Activities

weather observing   tax assistant
astronomy   computer games
reading   stamp collecting

Physical Activities

gardening

hiking

dancing

biking

tennis

cross country skiing

golf

aerobics

weight lifting

sailing

Creative Activities

flower arranging

cooking

wood carving

basket weaving

jewelry making

candle making

photography

calligraphy

pottery

musical instrument

Low Stress Activities

hammocking

fishing

bird feeding

art gallery watching

bird watching

High Adventure Activities

spelunking

sailing

rock climbing

motorcycle racing

treasure hunting

hot air ballooning

Crafting/Woodworking Activities

furniture making

wine making

farming or gardening

furniture repair

map making

furniture making

house painting

leather working

model aircraft making

Third, use a decision making grid to help you prioritize your leisure activities. For example:

Your Needs	**Potential Activities**			
	Skiing	Biking	Fishing	Hunting
Adventure	yes	yes	yes/no	yes
Low Cost	no	yes	yes	no
Social	yes	yes	yes/no	yes/no

You can see from this grid that biking best fits all three needs, fishing comes in second, skiing third and hunting fourth. Therefore, the most time now should be spent in biking with others.

Next, decide on the best time frame for leisure activities. Do you want to wait until later in the day or is early morning the best time for you? Try to find times during the day before the weekend. In general it is good to have a balance in your life which means having leisure activities come at various times during the day, rather than just an add on in the evenings or weekends.

Organizations

Thousands of organizations exist to help people learn or become more competent in their interests and hobbies. Among the more interesting ones are:

	Number of Members
American Bonanza Society	8,000
American Radio Relay League	161,000
Antique and Classic Boat Society	5,200
National Privy Diggers Association	95
Antique Doorknob Collectors of America	201
National Assoc. of Miniature Enthusiasts	13,000
National Button Society	3,400
The Mouse Club	2,000
Loyal Order of Catfish Lovers	3,000
National Scrabble Association	9,000
Escapees, Inc.	20,000
International Org. of Wooden Money Collectors	570
U. S. Boomerang Association	550
Association for the Study of Play	3,000

All of these organizations have newsletters and national meetings, so members never get bored.

Leisure Now

Are you tired of reading this book? Good, put it down and do something relaxing for a while. Go sit by a stream, take a walk around the neighborhood, listen to some music and relax. In fact I am going to stop here and go play with my kids for a while. BYE.

Learning

One of the greatest gifts that humans have is the capacity to learn relatively easily. Unfortunately, this gift is also one of the most underutilized. Because we were required to be in school for twelve to twenty years, many Americans feel burned out on prescribed learning. Yet, there are so many beautiful and fascinating things to learn in our world, it is a pity that we do not do more of it. If growth and success are to continue, it is important to learn or improve upon at least one skill a year.

LEARNING STYLES

Someone once told me that learning stopped after graduation from school, whether it be high school, college or graduate school. My response was that learning does not begin until after graduation. Unfortunately many people fail to recognize this and therefore do not progress very far in life. The first step in learning is to understand your personal preferred learning style. Learning styles can be grouped into five broad categories.

- Reading and Reflecting (R&R)
- Doing and Discussing (D&D)
- Creating and Constructing (C&C)
- Formal and Factual (F&F)

Which of these styles would you rank first, second, third and fourth for yourself? If you are not sure, review classes that were taken in school and decide which ones you liked best. What type of learning style was used in those classes? Throughout this book there will be many shortcuts based on learning style for your personal growth and career development.

Look for R&R, D&D, C&C or F&F next to these shortcuts and use those approaches if your personal learning style fits what is suggested. Everyone can profit from learning about the following during the next ten years.

- Using computers
- Different personality types and how to relate to them
- Making the most of your money
- How to avoid crime and violence
- Eating right
- Exercising properly
- Understanding people from other backgrounds
- Learning the history and cultures of other countries
- Understanding the differences between men and women

Gaining knowledge in these areas is not difficult. Hundreds of books are available on these topics. Additionally many courses are available on these topics through continuing education programs and employer sponsored training. Some of the most interesting courses I have seen recently include:

- A Brief History of Time
- Artificial Life
- Wilderness Survival
- Yoga and Meditation
- Total Relaxation
- Computers for the Complete Idiot
- The Fine Art of Small Talk
- Starting a Nonprofit Corporation
- How to Become a Tour Director
- Conversational French
- Basic Photography
- Classical Music for the Complete Idiot
- Art, Music and Great Ideas
- Illness Management
- Building High Self-Esteem
- 1001 Ways to Be Romantic
- Marrying Rich

What are your personal learning goals for the next twelve months?

1. _____
2. _____
3. _____
4. _____
5. _____

Additional Resources

Leisure Counseling. Arlin Epperson. C.C. Thomas, 1977.

National Avocational Organizations of the U.S. B. Klein Publications, 1986.

National Recreational, Sporting and Hobby Associations in the U.S. Craig Colgate & Regina Germain. Columbia Books, 1985.

Outdoor Idea Book. June Flemming. Victoria House, 1978.

Playfair: Everybody's Guide to Non Competitive Play. Matt Weinstein & Joel Goodman. Impact Publishers (dist.), 1980.

Recreation & Resources: Leisure Patterns and Leisure Places. Allan J. Pattman. Basil Blackwell, 1984.

Time to Spare. Lorraine H. Bailey. McGraw Hill, 1978.

What to Do After You Turn off the T.V. Francis Lappe. Ballentine Books, 1985.

8

VOLUNTEERING YOUR WAY TO SUCCESS

*I*n Ann Arbor, Michigan, Jane McCoy is the Program Director at a women's shelter that provides housing and services for battered women. Originally Jane volunteered for a year as the Front Desk Supervisor before being hired as Director. Mike Forrest is a Patient Care Assistant in the emergency room at Memorial Hospital in St. Louis. For Mike volunteering has not only meant helping others, but also given him valuable experience in real life and death situations. Sheryl Holmes volunteers four hours a week at the local humane society. Although happily employed as a Computer Analyst she feels that her volunteer work helps fulfill her lifelong need to care for animals. Ted Johnson, a retired geologist, volunteers at a paleontological museum located near dinosaur fossils. Ted says he loves to talk with second and third grade students who come to the museum. Volunteer situations similar to these are repeated thousands of times daily within the United States. Volunteering helps people feel needed, contributes to the welfare of others, promotes personal growth and facilitates employment. With all of these positive outcomes, nearly all of us can benefit from volunteer activities.

Volunteering To Help Others

Social service agencies, hospitals, libraries, and schools are popular places to volunteer. Agencies would not be able to provide many client services if volunteers were not available. Although no exact data is available, hundreds of thousands of people's lives have been improved by volunteers. President Clinton has proposed that college students pay off part of their federal loans through volunteer work during and after graduation as part of our new national agenda.

Volunteering For Personal Growth

Volunteering occurs not only because it helps others, but also because it facilitates our own growth and development. What areas of your life would you like to develop? Would you like to be a better listener, improve skills with children or the elderly; increase your ability to relate to adolescents; learn how to treat injured or abandoned animals; develop your teaching skills; or learn more about the environment and natural resources? Perhaps you would like to increase your knowledge of the arts, become involved in local political issues or help elderly people with home repairs. All of these skills can be learned or developed through volunteering a few hours a week.

Assistance can be provided in a multitude of ways.

- Direct people contact will allow you to work with individuals and listen to their concerns, provide advice and information or engage in therapeutic activities.

- The management level will give you an opportunity to work with other volunteers, coordinate events or programs, and develop your organizational and leadership skills.

- Want to develop your entrepreneurial skills? Try fund raising. All organizations these days need more money.

- As a volunteer researcher, you can develop your analytical skills and provide valuable information needed for program improvements.

- Perhaps you would like to use or develop your advertising and public relations skills. Most organizations have a need for individuals to conduct publicity including brochure development, press releases and posters.

VOLUNTEERING FOR CAREER DEVELOPMENT

Volunteering is an excellent way to investigate careers of interest. Improved career choices would be made if individuals tried out potential career options before making career decisions. After career choices have been narrowed to two or three options, volunteering can give the concrete experiences necessary to make solid decisions. Until this is done, career choices are merely assumptions, passions or imaginations of our mind. It is easily understandable why people have difficulty making career decisions if they have to do it without really experiencing the occupation. After volunteering in a position, if you are still uncertain about the "correctness" of an occupation, try a different agency. Clients, staff and policies vary greatly between organizations.

Volunteering frequently leads to paid job offers. Often organizations seek volunteers with the goal of hiring the brightest and most eager when paid positions occur. There is no better way to assess the skills of potential employees than by observing their work for several months. Volunteers with a great deal of initiative can even develop their own position by discovering a need in an organization and developing funding through internal or external sources.

Regardless of whether or not volunteering directly leads to a full time position, your employment candidacy will be strengthened by new skills learned, references obtained and enhancement of your resume. Additionally, it is easier to network with professionals from other agencies if you work within an established organization. You should volunteer in two or three agencies for fewer hours than in one for all of your time because you will become known by more people and position yourself better for openings that occur.

Having a clear understanding of responsibilities is important when beginning a volunteer position. Nothing is as frustrating to volunteers as assuming that they would do professional work and ending up answering the phone the majority of time. Also it is important to know the type and frequency of supervision, whom to discuss problems with, and written policies and procedures of the organization. Knowing the organizational structure and the roles and relationships of staff and other volunteers can also make your work much easier.

The amount of time available to volunteer varies from individual to individual. Some may volunteer several hours a week for many weeks while others might work on a special project that lasts a few days. If you are uncertain about the amount of time you have, start moderately because time commitments can always be increased and "free" employees are always in demand.

Volunteering with your children is an excellent way to develop their self-esteem, while at the same time conducting a family building experience. Allow your children to select volunteer sites from among options and try to keep the time duration short (e.g. 1-2 hours) until you assess their interests. Give your children an opportunity to reflect upon these experiences by asking such questions as, "What did you like or dislike about the work?" "What was learned about the place or people, and what did you learn about yourselves?"

Needs in Our Society

- An estimated 23 million Americans are illiterate or functionally illiterate.
- If current trends continue, the number of children living in poverty is estimated to increase 3 million by the year 2000.
- The number of citizens over age 80 will increase dramatically by the year 2000.
- It is estimated that before the year 2000, more than half of our cities will have exhausted their landfill capacities.
- Crime runs rampant in most large cities.

Volunteer Bank Account

People who someday may need rides to the doctor or help shoveling snow can volunteer to perform such work for elderly people and "bank" the credit. Those trying to care for elderly relatives in distant cities could trade their services. Doing volunteer work in their communities in exchange for help for family members in their own home towns. The Rocky Mountain HMO based in Grand Junction has begun such a pilot project through a grant from the Robert Wood Johnson Foundation.

With families more distant than they used to be, many people do not have relatives nearby to help with routine daily living. Locally, it can allow individuals taking care of elderly relatives an opportunity to volunteer somewhere else in exchange for another individual caring for relatives for a few hours.

The goal among organizers is to make the program available nationwide and independent of any HMO. "Its not expensive to run, said Dr. Vic Crumbaker, of the Rocky Mountain HMO, and would be the same mechanism that runs blood banks. You can give blood anywhere and it is available for you or anyone you select anywhere else."

LOCATING VOLUNTEER OPPORTUNITIES

Local Opportunities

Most medium to large sized cities have Volunteer Resource Centers. The purpose of these centers is to coordinate volunteers for a wide range of service agencies. Start with this type of agency because of array of opportunities they have is high. If no volunteer center is located in your town, try to locate a published directory that describes organizations of interest to you. United Way publishes this type of directory in many cities. If you cannot find the type of directory needed, call agencies directly and ask for information about their volunteer programs. Important information to gather includes type of volunteer positions and major duties, training received, number of volunteers, time requirements, and application process.

A Federal government agency in your area may also have volunteer opportunities (e.g. Bureau of Land Management), so also contact them. Experiences and supervision in federal agencies is usually excellent. Additionally, some local businesses may offer volunteer opportunities.

National Volunteer Opportunities

Many volunteer opportunities exist within national organizations. Some of the best volunteer programs include:

Art Job Bank, (505) 988-1166
City Volunteer Corps, (212) 475-6444
Coalition for the Homeless, (202) 328-1186
Community Jobs, (617) 720-5627
National Recreation and Parks, (703) 820-4920
The Nature Conservancy, (303) 444-1060
Student Conservation Association, (603) 543-1700
U.S. Bureau of Land Management, (303) 239-3669

U.S. Forest Service, (503) 326-3816
VISTA, (202) 634-9135

International Volunteer Opportunities

Amigos de las Americas, (713) 782-5290
Archaeology Abroad, 31-34 Gordon Square,
    London WC1H OPY, England
Club de Vieux Manoir, Paris, phone (33-14) 45.08.80.40
Council on International Educational Exchange, (212) 661-1414
Earthwatch, (617) 926-8200
Fourth World Movement, (301) 336-9489
Global Volunteers, (612) 228-9751
Health Volunteers Overseas, (202) 296-0928
Institute of Cultural Arts, (312) 769-6363
International Voluntary Service, (202) 387-5533
International Workcamper, (802) 259-2922
Partners of the Americas, (202) 628-3300
Peace Corps, (800) 424-8580

Recommended Readings

Directory of Volunteer Opportunities. Career Services, University of Waterloo. Waterloo, Ontario, 1992.

Good Works. A Guide to Careers in Social Change. Jessica Cowan. Barricade Books, 1991.

Non-Profits Job Finder. Daniel Lauber. Planning Communications, 1992.

Profitable Careers in Nonprofit. William Lewis and Carol Milano. John Wiley and Sons, 1987.

The International Directory of Volunteer Work. David Woodworth. Vacation Work, Peterson's Guides, 1989.

U.S. Nonprofit Organizations in Development Assistance Abroad. Wynta Boynes. Technical Assistance Information Clearinghouse. New York, 1983.

Volunteer. Council on International Educational Exchange. New York, 1990.

9

FUTURE TRENDS
AND YOUR SUCCESS

*T*he year was 1958 and Bob Johnson had just opened a sewing machine factory in Cleveland. The same year in Detroit, the Hanner family opened a neighborhood drug store. Less than ten years later both businesses were gone—due to changes in our society. To succeed in our rapidly transitioning country, it is important to be aware of major movements and their potential effect on your life. Five years ago no one predicted the decline for aerospace engineers nor the growth industry of software engineers in India. Ten years ago, no one predicted the slide of the automobile industry, but prices were growing ten to twelve percent a year! Accurately predicting change is not simple. Research has shown occupational projections to be only 60-65 percent accurate with national predictions more accurate than local ones.

SOCIETAL TRENDS

TREND 1: Increased Specialization of Most Products and Services

Product development and marketing has become increasingly specialized in recent years. For example, Coors Brewing Company in Colorado has recently come out with a product directed toward blue collar workers who drink more than twelve beers a week. They already have beers for professionals who drink fewer than six beers a week and brews for non-beer drinkers. Specialized marketing is promoted through individualized advertisements in national magazines modified for the area of the country or socioeconomic area of a city where the publication is delivered.

How many types of athletic shoes, writing pens, computers, automobiles, coffee, cereals, golf clubs, toothpastes, T.V. channels, sports events, and magazines can we choose from in our society? Options have multiplied dramatically over the past several years and will continue to do so with increasing frequency. Why has this specialization mushroomed and what supports it? Obviously people do not demand one hundred different types of automobiles or coffees. No legislation has been passed mandating twenty-eight types of toothpaste. What has occurred is competition among manufacturers to develop an edge for their products, and new companies looking for a market niche. Health needs did play a role in some medical and nutritional developments, but not for sixty eight different flavors of ice cream. This trend may continue to the point that soon cars will be individually designed as frequently as clothing.

This specialization of products and services will, of course, influence occupational development. Greater specialization will occur in the medical, legal and scientific fields as the body of knowledge that must be mastered to excel in a particular profession eliminates generalists. Also, individuals without advancement opportunities will further their careers by becoming specialists. Corporations will hire independent contractors and consultants with specialized knowledge in narrow fields.

TREND 2: Average Age of Population Getting Older

In 1981 there were 36 million Americans over 60 years of age. By 2031 that number will double. Accordingly, there will be a greater demand for development of products and services for people over 60. Athletic equipment, automobiles, computers, and many other products will be tailored to this group. Service opportunities will increase to assist older people who desire to continue an active lifestyle. Medical advances will treat some of the most prevalent diseases of this age group. Increased conflict may occur between younger people who want their share of society's wealth and older ones who feel they have already earned it.

TREND 3: Increased Cultural Diversity in the U.S.

The United States is the most ethnically diverse country in the world. About 32 million Americans now consider English a "foreign language." By the year 2000, one in every three Americans will be a minority. Additional emphasis will be given to differences in life style, education, work preferences, and health care for minorities. Multicultural consultants will be needed throughout our society.

TREND 4: Increased Concern for Environmental Issues

Major environmental problems such as air pollution, loss of forests, depletion of the ozone layer, toxic chemical waste, climate changes, and extinction will become even more acute. Waste disposal will become one of the major issues for large cities. Concern for indoor environment will increase including air quality, building materials, radon gas and communicable diseases.

TREND 5: Increased Global Interaction and World Economy

Although progress at times appears slow and uneven, we are truly moving to a world economy. No longer can the economic events in one part of the world be isolated from another. There is a world labor pool and American companies are using it. India has become the Silicon Valley of the world. Indian engineers, many of them trained in the U.S., are satisfied to work for $400-500 a month, which brings a high standard of living in that country. IBM, Hewlett Packard, Son Microsystems, Apple, Eastman Kodak and John Deere have major manufacturing bases in Europe. New markets are constantly opening up in the former Soviet Union. China, with its three billion population is a goldmine of opportunity for U.S. companies. Interdependence of national economies will rise as markets merge. National governments around the world will be selling off public services to private companies, many from the United States.

TREND 6: Rapid Advances in the Medical Field

Medical knowledge is doubling every eight years. Medical advances will give us artificial blood, spleens, lungs and skin. Human growth hormones and memory recall drugs will be developed. New computer based diagnostic tools will provide doctors with excellent images inside the body, thus eliminating the need for exploratory surgery. Brain cell and tissue transplants will occur early next century.

TREND 7: Continued Movement of U.S. Population from Northeast to South and West

The large northeastern cities will continue to decline in population. Crime, decay and loss of industrial jobs contribute to this decline. Life styles in the South and West will attract more residents. Areas of our country have growth and recessions at different times causing continuous migration.

TREND 8: Increased Use of Technology in Our Everyday Lives

How much time do you spend every day using machines—your automobile, telephone, computers, fax machines, television, stereo, VCR, microwave, etc. In this high tech society, we interact several hours each day with these mechanical companions. In fact technological advances have occurred much faster than humans' capacity to fully understand and use them (e.g. programming a VCR). What effect does this have on our society? Declining social skills, loss of real world experiences, decreased exercise, expectations that results can occur instantly, frustration when things are broken and we cannot fix them and greater friction between the people who can afford these items and ones who cannot. On the positive side, these technological improvements make life easier, information quicker to obtain and communication more effective. Home computers will grow rapidly as we access our mail, compare information on products and services, vote, complete income tax returns, and participate in educational programs. Interactive magazines and personalized newspapers with in- depth articles of the reader's choice will soon appear. "Smart pens" that can do a spell check as we write will soon be developed.

TREND 9: Expansion of Communication

Several years ago upon returning to work after a vacation, employees had only to answer written phone messages. Today we have to look at electronic mail, voice mail, faxed mail, and phone messages. Communications options are increasing dramatically. Soon we may be able to work anywhere in the world and also live wherever is pleasing.

These and other communications techniques will make offices almost obsolete.

TREND 10: Growing Need for Accurate Information

With all of the product and service options that are available, decision making becomes increasingly difficult. If more information were available, individuals could save thousands of dollars, many hours, and make better decisions. A national television network recently did a story on doctors' success rates for heart operations at a specific hospital. There was a large difference between physicians' success, but few people had this information. How can we make good decisions unless accurate information is easily available on housing, food, health care, vacations, gasoline, appliance and house repair, and automobiles. The technology exists to store and disseminate this information but the costs to gather and update it are enormous. By the year 2000 almost 40 percent of the labor force will be working in the information industry. IBM, NBC, and Numedia Corporation are test marketing a news-on-demand service for PC users.

TREND 11: Fewer and Fewer Meals Prepared at Home

Americans dine out like no other nation. Two-thirds of all meals are eaten out or carried out. More Americans than ever before eat their meals while driving. This has an effect not only on health but also social interaction of families.

TREND 12: Everyone Wants It Done Faster

Americans are very impatient. Everyone wants immediate results, and as technology develops, the pace of life quickens. Our societal structure will be modified by this need for speed. Only organizations that can speed up their products and services will survive and prosper. Activities that take a long time will disappear. Colleges will no longer have four years to educate students. Politicians will have less time to perform miracles or be voted out of office. The age of two term presidents is almost over. It took one hundred years to go from the agricultural to industrial age but only one fifth of that time to move into the information era. Major changes in the future may occur every five years or less.

TREND 13: A Widening Economic Gap in the U.S.

The number of middle class citizens will decrease while the ranks of rich and poor swell. This widening gap will cause increased crime in our country. Many poorer people will do whatever necessary to get the goodies. Political and social unrest will increase in the U.S.

TREND 14: A Growing Need to Reform Our Education System

The drop-out rate of high school students is increasing nationally and only 30 percent of those who graduate from high school complete college. Our educational system and students' learning styles are in conflict, but change is slow. Some students are very active learners and need to be doing rather than sitting and listening. Other students learn best by reading. Some students work best in groups rather than alone. Others need to be able to structure their own day. Our educational system is built upon educators' preferred teaching style rather than how students learn.

TREND 15: The U.S. Will Remain the Breadbasket of the World

As the world's population continues to explode at a rate of 91 million births a year, feeding our six billion population will become increasingly difficult. The United States remains the only country in the world with both natural resources and technology to produce much more food than it can consume. Transporting food throughout the world is our next challenge.

TREND 16: More Fathers Taking Primary Care Roles for Young Children

In 1977, 14 percent of fathers took care of young children; by 1991 the number was up to 20 percent. As changes occur in the work place more men are employed part time and women full time. Traditional home roles will continue to change.

GENERAL WORK FORCE TRENDS

TREND 1: Increased Part Time, Non-Permanent Employees

Full time permanent positions have become very difficult to obtain. More than 20 million professionals work part time in the U.S. About half of both professionals and non-professionals during the past year had part time or temporary work—up from twenty-five percent a decade ago. Many companies have adopted a form of work force management to compete in world markets. They keep a core of managers and valued workers and take on and shed others as business spurts and slumps.

TREND 2: Increase in Health Care Jobs

As our population ages and health care becomes available to everyone, the demand for health care will continue to grow. The need for home health aides, physical therapists, medical technicians, nurses, and medical assistants will grow considerably. Physician assistants will be able to prescribe drugs in 38 states by the year 2000. Seventeen states will authorize pharmacists to prescribe drugs. There will be a surplus of 100,000 physicians by 2001, thus more individual patient care. Prescriptions and treatment will be transmitted via computer.

TREND 3: Increase in Specialized Occupations

As information becomes more extensive and products become more specialized so will our work force. The history of occupational growth in our society is that most new occupations are specialized spin offs of traditional ones. Specialists in medicine, psychology, law, teaching, computerization, finances, real estate and other areas will increase. If you want to find a job with your degree, then develop a specialization that is unique and needed.

TREND 4: Increase in Service Jobs

One of the major complaints in our complex and busy society is lack of time to do everything. How can we deal with this lack of time? One way is to hire service providers. These people clean house, take care of pets, grocery shop, deliver children to activities, care for lawns and plants, take care of car repairs and many other tasks. Can't afford one?

Share one with a neighbor or cut back expenses in other areas. The Bureau of Labor Statistics predicts that by the year 2000, 85 percent of the labor force will be service workers. They probably will be called personal assistants and home care coordinators.

One million service jobs in manufacturing, transportation and agriculture will be created in the next decade. There will be a shortage of low wage service workers in restaurants, department stores, and other retail outlets.

TREND 5: Most Employment Opportunities Will Occur in Small to Medium Sized Companies

The average corporation today has only 200 employees. Predictions are that 60-80 percent of new employment opportunities will occur in small to medium sized companies of 500 employees or fewer. Most large companies are down sizing or not filling vacancies when employees retire. Benefits of working in small companies include flexibility of work style, informal atmosphere, greater opportunity for advancement, variety of tasks and "family feeling."

TREND 6: More Entrepreneurs

Between 1950 and 1986, the number of new businesses created annually grew from 100,000 to 700,000. More mid-career professionals will become entrepreneurs as their chances for promotion in organizations diminish. Women are starting small businesses as never before. Additionally, latchkey kids who grew up with one parent and had a great deal of autonomy do not want to work for organizations.

TREND 7: More People Working at Home

A major method for organizations to lower costs is to have less office space. In the future more employees will be working at home. With increased use of computers, modems and fax machines, more can be accomplished at home than in an office. This arrangement saves transportation, clothing and food costs for employees and heating, rental and maintenance expenses for employers.

TREND 8: More Minorities in the Work Force

Black workers made up 10.7 percent of the civilian labor force in

1985. By 1995, that number will have risen to 11.5 percent. Hispanic workers made up 7.2 percent of the labor force in 1992, up from 5.7 percent in 1980. By the year 2000, for the first time, white males will be in the minority of labor force entrants. IBM began the "Portable Officer Workstation Project" in August of 1992, with a goal of converting 180 marketing and sales staffers into remote employees working from their choice of private homes, customer offices, or a car. Employees were issued a 4886 color laptop computer, high speed fax/modem, a cellular phone with a modem interface and a portable, letter-quality printer. Annual expenses to IBM have been reduced by over $10 million a year.

TREND 9: Further Decline of Agricultural and Manufacturing Industries

There will be 900,000 fewer farmers in the U.S. in the year 2000. Between 1979 and 1985, 1.7 million manufacturing jobs disappeared. By the year 2000 the labor manufacturing force will account for only 9.7 percent of the total labor force, down from 18 percent in 1987. With the evolution of new materials, production technology, computer aided manufacturing and robotics, unskilled and semi-skilled jobs in manufacturing will almost disappear.

TREND 10: Elimination of Middle Management

Middle management positions will decline as information flows to higher management for analysis. Opportunities for advancement will decrease with more specialists at the bottom. Management styles will be more consultative and participatory rather than authoritative.

TREND 11: Decline in the Work Ethic

Tardiness increases and sick leave abuse is common. Job security, high pay and company loyalty are no longer the motivators they once were. Temporary employment results in employees thinking of themselves first.

USING TREND INFORMATION
TO ACHIEVE SUCCESS

How can this trend information be used by you in planning your future? First do a little exercise similar to the one below. Take out a sheet of paper and across the page(s) list your past accomplishments, both work related and personal. Second, down the left column of the page list all of the future trends mentioned in this chapter that may affect you and add one or two that may be going on in your state or city. Third, think of ways your accomplishments can be used within these trends and write them in next to the trends.

Accomplishments

(example) Trends	1	2	3	4
Aging Population				
Global Economy				
Need for Information				
Increased Specialization				
Environmental Issues				
Cultural Diversity				
Technology Boom				
Increase in Health Care & Service Jobs				
More Entrepreneurs				
Population Shift to South and West				
More People Working at Home				
Job Opportunities in Small Companies				

You may not be able to relate all of your accomplishments with future trends, but some will match. Matching your accomplishments with trends in our society increases chances of success. On the other hand, if you are primarily skilled to achieve in areas that are outdated, your growth may be limited. List four potential accomplishments that you would like to explore, that fit with these trends.

1. _____
2. _____
3. _____
4. _____

Short Range Occupational Projections

It is important to analyze both long and short range employment opportunities. Short range projections of course will have greater accuracy. Occupations that are expected to have rapid growth in the next ten years, according to the U.S. Department of Labor include:

Occupation	10 Year Percentage Increase
▪ Home Health Aides	92
▪ Paralegals	85
▪ Systems Analysts Computer Scientists	79
▪ Personal Home Care Aides	77
▪ Physical Therapists	76
▪ Medical Assistants	74
▪ Operations Research Analysts	74
▪ Human Service Workers	71
▪ Radiological Technicians	70
▪ Medical Secretaries	68
▪ Psychologists	64
▪ Travel Agents	62
▪ Corrections Officers	61
▪ Computer Equipment Repairers	60
▪ Occupational Therapists	55
▪ Management Analysts	52
▪ Registered Nurses	44
▪ Accountants/Auditors	35
▪ Lawyers	35
▪ Teachers	24
▪ Retail Sales	24

Occupations with the projected largest decline 1990-2005 include:

Occupation	Projected Percentage Decline
▪ Central Office Operators	59
▪ Electronic Assemblers	47
▪ PBX Installers/Repairers	42
▪ Child Care Workers	40
▪ Statistical Clerks	36
▪ Textile Operators	31
▪ Household Cleaners	25
▪ Machinists	25

U.S. News and World Report in November, 1993 stated that the hottest tracks in professions were:

- ▪ Medicine—Geriatrician
- ▪ Personal Service—Home Care Aide
- ▪ Sales—Business Services
- ▪ Scientific Research—Protein Chemist
- ▪ Social Work—Employee Assistance
- ▪ Telecommunications—Telecommunications Manager
- ▪ Education—Bilingual Education Teacher
- ▪ Engineering—Computer Software Engineer
- ▪ Environment—Environmental Engineer
- ▪ Environment—Environmental Lawyer
- ▪ Media—Cable Ad Sales Rep

Industrial Growth

Industrial growth shows mixed predictions for the next two years according to highlights from the 1993 U.S. Industrial Outlook report. The ten fastest growing industries for 1992-93 were:

- ▪ Semiconductors — 12.0%
- ▪ Surgical and Medical Instruments — 8.5%
- ▪ Surgical Appliances and Supplies — 8.5%
- ▪ Computers and Peripherals — 8.2%
- ▪ Electromedical Equipment — 7.8%
- ▪ Motor Vehicles — 6.8%
- ▪ Household Laundry Equipment — 6.7%
- ▪ Household Refrigerators and Freezers — 6.5%
- ▪ Automobile Parts and Accessories — 6.1%

- X-ray Apparatus and Tubes   5.6%

The ten slowest growing industries in 1992-93 were:

- Aircraft   -6.0%
- Space Vehicle Equipment   -6.0%
- Guided Missiles and Space Vehicles   -5.7%
- Paper Industries Machinery   -5.2%
- Space Propulsion Units and Parts   -5.0%
- Aircraft Parts and Equipment   -4.8%
- Aircraft Engines and Parts   -3.8%
- Leather and Sheep Lines Clothing   -3.8%
- Women's Handbags and Purses   -3.6%
- Personal Leather Goods   -3.4%

Growth in service industries tends to outshine manufacturing and some of the highest acceleration in 1992-93 include the following groups:

- Venture Capitol   28.0%
- Electronic Information Services   16.4%
- Data Processing   13.7%
- Health Services   12.1%
- Prerecorded Music   11.3%
- Computer Professional Services   9.3%
- Credit Unions   8.0%
- Home Entertainment   7.7%
- Apparel Sales   7.1%
- Restaurant Help   6.8%
- Legal Services   6.5%
- Telecommunications   6.3%
- Travel Services   5.7%
- Management Consulting   5.3%
- Equipment Leasing   5.0%
- Property/Casualty Insurance   4.0%

Additional Resources

American Industry Annual Report. Forbes Magazine, 1993.

CAM Report: Career Movement and Management Facts. Priam Publications, East Lansing, MI, 1993.

Outlook 1990-2005. U.S. Department of Labor, Bureau of Labor Statistics, 1989.

What Lies Ahead: Countdown to the 21st Century. United Way of America, 1990.

The Futurist. World Future Society, Bethesda, MD.

U.S. Industrial Outlook 1993. U.S. Department of Commerce. International Trade Administration, 1992.

Work in America: the Decade Ahead. Clark Kerr and Jerome M. Rostow. Van Nostrand, 1979.

10

FORGET CAREERS, DO HOBBYJOB PLANNING

*Y*ou know its time to change your career when. . .

- You spend more money buying lottery tickets than improving your work skills;
- You are unemployed more than employed;
- Weekends are more enjoyable than the work week;
- You despise office meetings;
- Golf has more challenge than your work;
- You dislike talking about your work;
- At work you try to do the easiest job possible.

CAREER CHOICES

Many individuals make career changes because their initial choice was poor. How do people really make their initial career choice? Well not surprisingly it usually is not based on logic or information. Careers are chosen because:

- Good job opportunities appear available in that career.

- In college, they majored in an academic area that is directly associated with the career.
- High financial rewards are associated with the work.
- Friends or siblings chose that direction.
- Parents had similar occupations.
- Parents directly or indirectly told them what they could and could not pursue.
- Their geographical location influenced career knowledge and choice (e.g. very few fishermen from Nevada).
- Occupational stereotypes influenced their decision.
- With the help of a friend or spouse, they fell into something.
- They chose something quickly to answer the nagging question of "what are you going to do when you grow up?"

All of this implies, of course, that people do not make career decisions solely based upon their own needs, values and interests, which is usually true. At the time we make our first career decisions, we are very young and influenceable. Career changes in our thirties and forties are less influenced by the other factors and based more on our own needs and skills.

CAREER AVOIDANCE STRATEGIES

Many excellent strategies exist to AVOID making career plans:

- **Hoping career tests will tell you what to do.** Career tests cannot tell you what to do, only your mother, father or boss will do that. Career tests can give you options and ideas of potential directions. Guess who has to make the final decision?

- **Hoping one day that you will wake up and know which direction to pursue.** Wouldn't it be nice if you could wake up tomorrow with the answer to your career concerns? Unfortunately it is not that easy. You might go to sleep tomorrow night and come up with a different career and still be confused.

- **Letting fate decide your career direction.** Many people believe that they have little influence in their career direction, therefore they should let fate play its proper role. Fate does play a role in all of our lives, and particularly in career planning, but we should let it come in the front door while we are awake, and not the back door while we are sleeping. In other words we should first decide on the general direction (e.g. business) we would like to proceed and then let fate support that direction (e.g. sales).

- **A career counselor will tell you what direction to pursue.** Everyone, including career counselors have biases and limited experiences, therefore be careful when career counselors over-direct you. The best career counselors listen to your needs and give suggestions of potential directions, both career and non-career related.

- **Going where the opportunities exist.** Unfortunately, there are many well employed and unhappy professionals. Yes, it is important to know where the opportunities are but they must also fit your interests, or a career change will occur within three to five years. Also, the demand for specific occupations may be high one year and three years later drop, and you may become both unemployed and unhappy.

HOBBYJOBS

Many people love their hobbies and have a mild like for their jobs. Why not then make your job a hobby or turn your hobby into a job. What is the difference between hobbies and jobs?

- Hobbies are fun and jobs are work. Try to get more fun out of your work by seeing the humorous sides and doing enjoyable aspects more often.

- Continuous learning occurs in hobbies making them stimulating. How much learning are you doing in your job and how might it be increased?

- New gadgets are constantly being purchased for our hobbies to add interest. What new additions have been recently included at your work to increase your interest (e.g.

computers, furniture, redecoration)?

- Many clubs and organizations are available for people to share hobbies. With whom do you share work-related interests?

- People often have several hobbies at once therefore avoiding boredom. Can you have variety with your work or several jobs?

- People usually do not engage in hobbies that are life or death situations. Does your job feel extremely intense? Is this real or imaginary and how much pressure do you put on yourself?

- Hobbies can be left alone for periods of time when boredom occurs. How often do you take vacations from your work?

While still very young, Jack Fredericks committed himself to a degree in accounting because of skills solving financial problems. Although Jack found the monetary rewards excellent, he was frustrated by being limited in not using all of his interests in his work. Music was Jack's hobby and he also liked wood working. As a challenge from a friend, Jack built a guitar. From this first attempt, he learned so much that he tried it again. The second guitar sold for the cost of materials while the third one brought $500 profit. Jack now devotes full time to guitar building, charging $3000 for each instrument, and has a three year waiting list of customers.

Characteristics of Successful Hobbyjobs

Hobbyjobs are fun! Ask most employees how much fun they have at work and they usually will say they have fun less than 20 percent of the time. Many Americans try to make their work fun but are unsuccessful. Ask doctors, lawyers and other professionals how much fun they have in their work and you will hear that it is minimal. Does work have to involve difficult and intense tasks all day long? Not if you have a hobbyjob. Hobbyjobbers enjoy going to work, smile a lot and have fun 50-60 percent of the time. How often do you have fun at work?

List three things you can do to have more fun at work.

   1. _____
   2. _____
   3. _____

Work is an Extension of Their Personality

While it is true that careerists can inject their personality into work, most of them do it only minimally. Have you ever heard the statement that we are "one person at work and another at home." This is the true sign of a careerist. Observe people who work in law firms, financial institutions, government agencies, etc. . . Do you think that they behave the same way at home? Hardly, or their spouses, children and pets would disown them. A hobbyjobber can be natural at work, wear comfortable clothes, behave normally and fulfill personal needs.

Hobbyjobbers Have More
Freedom in Their Work

Have you ever wanted to skip a meeting because you knew it would be a waste of time, but felt you **had to go**. Careerists frequently end up in non-productive meetings because it would be unacceptable in their organization to do otherwise. Hobbyjobbers are wiser. If a meeting is not worthwhile, they find a valid way out. Hobbyjobbers also have more control over their work day and maintain flexible work schedules.

Hobbyjobbers Keep a Balance in Life and Obtain
as Much Satisfaction Outside of Work as During Work Hours

How often do you work overtime in the evening and weekends? Hobbyjobbers work diligently at their job during the assigned work hours but rarely work overtime unless they want to. Balance is essential in their lives and they know if work consumes 50-60 hours a week, there will be little energy left for outside interests. The work performance of hobbyjobbers is no lower than careerists, they just use their time more efficiently. By obtaining satisfaction from interests outside of work, hobbyjobbers can come to work more refreshed and enthusiastic.

Hobbyjobbers Are Their Own Boss
and Primarily Work For Themselves

Supervisors give employees fits by commenting on everything at work, and even personal life. Many supervisors do not have "super-vision" and in fact are nearsighted. Hobbyjobbers either work for themselves or do a good job of managing their supervisors. They have learned to be dedicated workers and assertive with supervisors, which garners respect and freedom.

Hobbyjobbers Work Out of Enjoyment, Not Fear

Many individual's work is driven by fear. This can be fear of failure, fear of losing their jobs, fear of not being able to pay their bills, fear of being seen as a failure by others, or losing the lifestyle they desire. This phobia, like most fears is irrational. Very few ambitious people in our society will ever starve or be homeless. Hobbyjobbers accept the fact that there will be both good and bad times, and enjoy all aspects of their lives. When work related success is not occurring, they find fulfillment elsewhere. Careerists feel that if they are not advancing in their work, they are failing.

Hobbyjobbers Enjoy Their Current Position in Life

Constantly looking to the future is the sign of a careerist. In their looking they hope for advancement, vacations and retirement rather than enjoying their work now. Hobbyjobbers enjoy the present moment, their co-workers and the work. They know if advancement is to come, it will happen because of who they are and their quality of work, not through politicking.

HEARTJOBS

Do you really have a compassion for someone or something? Is it animals, the homeless, children, the elderly, immigrants, people in third world nations?

Use the chart below to help you in deciding the level of compassions:

| | **Interest** | |
	High	Medium	Low

Group

Elderly
Homeless
Poor
Illiterate
Immigrants
Adopted
Children
Disabled
Third World
Religious Group
Cats
Dogs
Other Animals

Susan had been a social worker in a variety of agencies for eight years. During the last four years she worked for an adoption agency but disliked the legal issues, interpersonal conflicts and paperwork. When Susan's young cat died, she volunteered in an animal shelter. In two weeks she soon fell in love with the animals and quit her social work job. Susan now is director of adoption for the animals at the shelter. Her long term goal is animal shelter consulting and teaching.

Many heartjob occupations exist. Obtain information about them from the following resources:

Careers for Good Samaritans and Other Humanitarian Types

Careers for Animal Lovers and Other Zoological Types

Good Works: a Guide to Social Change Careers

Green at Work

State Social Services Agency Directories

HOMEJOBS

Rather than working in an office, many people prefer homejobs. Office presence used to have more status than working at home, even though thousands of dollars and many traveling hours were spent. With use of computers and rising costs of office space, increasing numbers of employers and employees will choose homework in the future.

NOJOB

Let's be honest, some people prefer not to work at all. There is no reason to ignore or feel bad about this as long as you can find an honest way to survive. Jeff Olmsted made good investments that allowed him to retire at the rather early age of 47. Frequently he attended social events where business cards were exchanged. To avoid feeling out of place he developed his own card which said the following:

```
┌──────────────────────────────────────────────┐
│                                                │
│     Hiking                    Sailing          │
│                                                │
│                Jeff Olmsted                    │
│               Investor, retired                │
│                  671-3429                      │
│                                                │
│     Tennis                    Golf             │
└──────────────────────────────────────────────┘
```

What would your nojob card look like?

We all need to develop a balance between or hobbyjobs, heartjobs, homejobs and nojobs. In the space below describe your balance in these areas.

Hours Per Week

Hobbyjob:
Heartjob:
Homejob:
Nojob:

Working Patterns

In the 1950's through 1970's there were very few opportunities to stylize a career. People usually had their own business or a full time job within an organization, and stayed with it for much of their lives. The 1980's saw a few variations on this pattern, such as job sharing. Dramatic varieties of career styles will develop in the next few years with many options. People will design their own working patterns to fit their needs. Some of the most popular working patterns will be the following:

Several Part Time Positions

People in these types of positions work at several different employment sites and at home. Beth is a counselor who helps clients with both career and personal concerns. She works part time at a women's counseling center, a state employment agency, consults and does private practice at home. She admits, "I love the variety that these positions offer and do not feel trapped in one office."

The Seventy Percenter

Many individuals no longer work a full forty hour week but rather 25-30 hours. This saves organizations from having to pay benefits and allows individuals time for outside interests. Carole is an accountant at a major clothing manufacturer in Cleveland. She is divorced and has one child 27 years old. To fulfill her nurturing needs, Carole volunteered to be on the board of directors at a local animal shelter. Her thirty hours a week position allows time for a volunteer commitment and brings balance to her life.

Major and Minor Careers

Frequently, while in college, students have both a major and minor area of study. Why not also have this in your work. John is an engineer in a small manufacturing company and has a minor career as a weekend musician. An accountant during the week, Kathy has a good cart at sports events on the weekends.

What types of minor career might be interesting to you? Ideally, they would be fun, different from your regular work, allow you to express other sides of your personality and permit you to interact with people outside of your major career.

Three Years Work, One Year Play

Who said that we must work all of our adult lives? Taking time off every few years can greatly revitalize ourselves and help us learn. Robert was a finance officer at a large bank in Chicago. After five years in the position he was burned out. Robert took two years off to work on an MBA and is now Vice President for finance at a bank in Portland. While his time off wasn't exactly play, he recharged his intellectual batteries and returned to work newly energized. "I grew a great deal from that time off and am now planning my next sabbatical."

Needs and Careers

Need fulfillment is the basis of career choice. Needs may be clearly understood by an individual or they might be subconscious in nature. If you are aware of your needs, choose an occupation that best fits them. Work satisfaction is dependant upon the extent that an occupation can fulfill needs. Some examples of occupations and needs are:

Occupation	Needs Fulfilled
Teachers	Working with children Encouraging growth • Autonomy Nurturing Conformity Affiliation Non-aggressiveness
Nurses	Order Nurturing Introversion
Artists	Lack of conflict Individuality Non-success pressure
Engineers	Stability Achievement Order Dominance

Lawyers	Achievement
	Affiliation
	Dominance
Accountants	Correctness
	Emotional control
	Order
Business people	Pragmatism
	Dominance
	Aggressiveness

DISCOVERING YOUR HOBBYJOB STYLE

Enjoyable hobbyjobs do not just happen, they must be planned. Talk with people who have successful hobbyjobs and you will notice careful planning and goal setting. The same must be done by you or the result might be a boring job. Finding a satisfying hobbyjob is not difficult if you complete the following steps.

1. Self Assessment
2. Reading Occupational Information
3. Experiencing Options
4. Decision Making
5. Planning Next Steps

Self Assessment

The first step in good planning is to analyze needs, interests, values and skills. You should be able to answer the following questions.

1. What am I good at and what skills do I have?
2. Which skills would I enjoy using?
3. What kind of people do I like be around?
4. What would I like to accomplish at work?
5. How much responsibility would I like?
6. Where in the U.S. or abroad would I like to work?
7. For what type of organization would I like to work?
8. Would I prefer to have my own business?
9. Would I prefer to be a specialist or have a wide variety of duties?

These are just a few of the questions that will help you clarify a hobbyjob for yourself.

To initiate your hobbyjob planning, first, take a day off from work, sleep late, read the paper and listen to your favorite music. Find a quiet place in your house, the woods, nearby mountains, a stream or ocean. If possible, go on a vacation for a few days. Complete the following exercises.

Exercise #1—Enjoyable Activities

What do I enjoy doing in my leisure time?

play cards?

play sports?

go to parties?

read?

watch movies?

relax and daydream?

go hiking?

work in the garden?

crafts and woodworking?

travel?

play with my pets?

What types of hobbyjobs might fit these needs? Our leisure activities are not random but fulfill specific needs.

Exercise #2—Values Ranking

Tear a sheet of paper into 20 small pieces. On each piece write one of the following words:

advancement

* independence

* relaxed pace

friendships

* work environment

challenge

(leave two pieces blank)

adventure

leadership

security

prestige

leisure

teamwork

creativity

salary

* helping others

organization

making decisions

visibility

Now, turn all of the pieces over and mix them up. Pick up one piece at a time and place them in priority order. Each time you place a piece in priority order, your list may need slight rearrangement. On the two blank pieces, write some needs or values not on the list above? After prioritizing all 16 needs and values, take a few minutes to reflect on your list. Are you surprised by your most important needs and values? How many of your most important needs do you have in your current work? Which least important values also appear in your job? How would your parents, spouse, and supervisor prioritize these needs and values and does this influence you? Have your needs and values changed at all in the last few years? Is it possible to change your current work to include more of your needs?

Exercise #3—Ideal Job

If you could work at anything you wanted this next year and still earn $200,000, **where would you work?**

- Geographical location?
- Size of city?
- Large or small organization?
- Self employment?
- Indoors or outside?

What kinds of people would be your co-workers?

- Creative people?
- Social people?
- Task oriented?
- Easy going?

What tasks or duties would you be doing?

What types of rewards would you get from your work?

- Helping people?
- Recognition?
- Creating or developing new ideas?

What would your typical day be like?

- Would you be managing people?
- Managed?
- Work alone?

What does this say to you about your needs in a hobbyjob? How much of this ideal do you have in your current work?

My Needs in a Career	What is Being Met Currently
1. _____	1. _____
2. _____	2. _____
3. _____	3. _____
4. _____	4. _____
5. _____	5. _____

If you are very satisfied with your current work, your ideal job probably closely matches your current position. If you are dissatisfied, your current position is likely very different from your ideal hobbyjob.

Exercise #4—Analyzing Past Experiences

Review current and past positions and other relevant experiences. You can learn a great deal about yourself from past experiences if sufficient time is given to reviewing and understanding them. The most important self information is right in front of us if we choose to use it. Describe at least four work, volunteer, recreational or other activities in which you have spent a significant amount of time and energy. Describe the activity, what you liked most and least. Follow the example below:

Activity	Likes	Dislikes
Accounting job	Co-workers Atmosphere	Detail Overtime
Part time teaching	Students Learning	Discipline Preparation
Organizing neighborhood voter registration	Meeting people Co-workers	Late hours
Reading	Learning new ideas Relaxing	Isolation

After you have finished this exercise, review your likes and dislikes for patterns or themes. What do these themes say to you about your needs?

Exercise #5—Life Development

If you had several lives to live and had to have a different occupation in each life, what would you do?

1st life— _____
2nd life— _____
3rd life— _____
4th life— _____

What does this say to you about your interests and potential, life development and hobbyjob growth?

Exercise #6—Past Accomplishments

Review your accomplishments from chapter two. What do these accomplishments say about your needs and values? What types of work might allow you to achieve these accomplishments?

Exercise #7—People Qualities

In the columns below, list qualities liked and disliked about people, values expressed and potential occupations.

Like About People (example)	Dislike	Values Expressed	Potential Occupations
Outgoing, upbeat	Reserved	Extroversion	Sales
Supportive	Competitive	Helping	Counseling, teaching

Exercise #7—Switching Careers

Describe three people with whom you would exchange careers. They can be acquaintances or people you know distantly.

Person	Job Duties	Values and Skills Used in Work
1. _____	_____	_____
2. _____	_____	_____
3. _____	_____	_____

Now that you have completed these exercises, what do they reveal about your needs and values?

1. Most important needs and values
2. Moderately important needs and values
3. Least important needs and values

Can you think of three to five types of work or hobbyjobs that might fit these needs?

1. _____
2. _____
3. _____
4. _____
5. _____

Obtaining Information

The second step in good hobbyjob planning is to obtain quality information about the work or volunteer activity options you are considering. This can be accomplished by reading information about occupations, using computerized career guidance systems, talking with people working in areas of interest to you, and attending career workshops or seminars.

Informational Interviewing

Seek out and talk with people in hobbyjobs. You should be able to spot them rather easily. They smile at work and enjoy life. Talk to these people about their work including how they "got there," what they like and dislike about it, their rewards, risks taken to be where they are, dealing with financial insecurity, what significant others said about their career changes and how they dealt with those people, and any other questions you may have.

Reading Occupational Information

Discovering potential hobbyjobs can also be initiated by reading related written information. Most people make career decisions based on very limited occupational information. Individuals who grew up in the 1950's or earlier, or lived in small cities had limited occupational information and usually relied on a few role models to discover career options. Review the recommended readings at the end of this chapter for suggested types of work.

Experiencing Options

The third step in finding a satisfying hobbyjob is trying out desirable options. Important decisions can be made easier by testing the options first. Would you purchase an automobile without driving it first? Would you marry someone without dating him or her first? Many people still try to make a career decision based upon limited information and misinformation, rather than experiences. Several ways to experience an occupation include: volunteering one or two days a week or for special projects with a hobbyjobber. Learn as much as possible about job duties, skills needed, training opportunities, tools or equipment required, community resources, dress codes, communication styles, work patterns, and how to obtain a paid position. Be eager, volunteer to help in any way possible and take initiatives and additional responsibilities. Internship programs are readily available for high school and college students but difficult for adults to obtain. Visit a local college's internship office, preferably one that has many adult students, and inquire about internship opportunities. If it is required to be a student, it may be worthwhile to sign up for one or two classes. You will find the available internship opportunities outstanding and helpful making decisions.

After experiencing some hobbyjobs, some options will stand out and others become less appealing. If several options appeal to you, do not worry. You may enjoy doing one for a few years and another later. Also, the opportunities may be greater in one area than another. The decision making grid below can help you decide on options.

Decision Making

At some point it will be necessary to decide upon a hobbyjob direction. If adequate time has been devoted to self assessment, reading information, talking with people and testing out options, hobbyjob decisions can be easier. The decision making grid described below can be very useful in making any decision.

In the left column, write in all options you are considering. Across the top of the page write in all of the factors that it is important for you to consider (e.g. salary, opportunities, enjoyment, additional skills needed). Rate each factor as high medium or low for each hobbyjob option. Review the decision making grid to see if certain options rise above others.

Important Factors to Consider
(Your List)

examples
Opportunities Salary Enjoyment Training Needed

Hobbyjob Options
1. _____
2. _____
3. _____
4. _____
5. _____

Planning Next Steps

It is important to plan the next steps in your hobbyjob search.

- What would you like to accomplish this next week?
- What do you need to do to achieve this accomplishment?
- What barriers might hinder you?
- How can you get around these barriers?
- Who can help you achieve these goals?

After the first week, you should repeat this exercise until you are well under way towards a desired direction.

Choosing An Adequate Time Span

In order to change a career direction, it is important to dedicate enough time to implement the decision. Usually career changers devote six months to two years for implementation depending on the type of financial and social support that is available. If, at the end of the time span selected, goals are close at hand, additional time should be taken. On the other hand, if at the end the allotted time you are not very far along, it may be wisest to return to your previous way of making a living and assess what has been learned or modify your previous work style. Which time frame for implementing your new career style do you feel would work best for you and why?

- One to six months
- One to twelve months
- One to twenty-four months

The advantage of having a set time frame rather than just "seeing what happens" is that it puts some pressure on you to move ahead. At some point it will be necessary to discuss your plans with your employer and family. Frequently employers will agree to reduce your hours and/or give a leave of absence if the timing is right. Make sure you obtain an agreement in writing stating the date you intend to return.

Shortcutting the Process

Sometimes people say that the process described above takes too much time and work. If you truly feel that way, try one of the techniques described below.

- If you are a very social person, do mostly informational interviews with people employed in occupations of interest.
- If you enjoy research, read information about work of interest and pay careful attention to job duties, work environments, educational requirements, salary and employment outlook.
- If you consider yourself a very active person, try out several types of appealing work.
- If you would rather work for yourself, start a small business and see where it leads.
- If you are a creative person, find a hobbyjob that has low demands and will allow you to retain energy for other interests.

Other Resources, Tests, Computer Systems

Several other resources exist to help you explore options.

- Career counselors are available through colleges and social service agencies, at low cost. Make sure these counselors understand you are not seeking a traditional career direction and help you discover creative options.

- Career tests such as the *Self Directed Search* and the *Strong Campbell Interest Inventory* can help you decide on career directions. One word of caution, most career tests provide lists of very traditional careers. Therefore to use career tests in hobbyjob planning, you must creatively brainstorm "spin off" career styles options for yourself.

- Computer systems are also available through high schools and colleges and can provide you a great deal of information about work options.

Additional Resources

Career Planning and Development for College Students and Recent Graduates. John E. Steele and Marilyn S. Morgan VGM Career Horizons, 1991.

Offbeat Careers: The Directory of Unusual Work. Al Sacharov. Ten Speed Press, 1988.

Re-Careering in Turbulent Times. Ronald L. Krannich. Impact Publications, 1983.

The Complete Job Search Handbook. Howard Figler. Henry Holt and Company, 1988.

The 1993 What Color Is Your Parachute. Richard N. Bolles. Ten Speed Press, 1993.

Wishcraft. Barbara Scher. Ballentine Books, 1979.

11

DICTIONARY OF PAINFUL PROFESSIONAL OCCUPATIONS (DOPPOS)

*H*undreds of occupations exist that support personal growth. On the other hand there are many occupations that will drain your energy, provide frustrations, and inhibit non-work achievements. Before describing these positions, let's examine the U.S. occupational structure will be given.

The U.S. Office of Education (U.S.O.E.) lists fifteen broad areas of occupations including:

1. Business and Office (e.g. data processor, bookkeeper, accountant, file clerk)
2. Marketing and Distribution (e.g. salesperson, marketing researcher, economist, systems analyst)
3. Communications and Media (e.g. reporter, photoengraver, script writer, electronic technician)
4. Construction (e.g. architect, paperhanger, bricklayer, roofer, plasterer)
5. Manufacturing (e.g. machine operator, chemist, welder, tool and die maker)
6. Transportation (e.g. pilot, truck driver, auto mechanic, aerospace engineer)

7. Agribusiness and Natural Resources (e.g. farmer, miner, farm agent, wildlife management)
8. Marine Science (e.g. diver, fisherperson, marine biologist)
9. Environment (e.g. forest ranger, meteorologist, geologist, tree surgeon)
10. Public Services (e.g. counselor, fireperson, policeperson, probation officer)
11. Health (e.g. psychologist, veterinarian, dentist, speech pathologist, chiropractor)
12. Recreation and Hospitality (e.g. waitress, chef, golf pro, hotel manager)
13. Personal Services (e.g. beautician, priest, mortician, TV repairperson)
14. Fine Arts and Humanities (e.g. dancer, author, jeweler, piano tuner)
15. Consumer and Homemaking Education (e.g. interior decorator, seamstress, model)

Some areas of the U.S.O.E. categories are better suited for enjoyable career styles while others will require intense work commitments. Most of the business and office, marketing and distribution, manufacturing, construction, public services, transportation, communications and media, personal services and health are very demanding in terms of stress, long work hours and lower rewards. On the other hand, natural resources, marine science, environment, recreation and hospitality, and fine arts support flexible career styles and non-work activities.

Painful	Enjoyable
public services	natural resources
media, sales	fine arts
business and office	marine science
construction	recreation
transportation	hospitality

SATISFYING OCCUPATIONS

Recently, *Money Magazine* surveyed individuals employed in a variety of occupations to assess satisfaction with their work. The following results were discovered:

Individuals Who Felt Excellent Satisfaction

biologists	chemists
geologists	electrical engineers
sociologists	bank officers
urban planners	aeronautical engineers
civil engineers	computer analyst

Those Who Felt Good Satisfaction Included

college math teacher	architect
high school principal	librarian
pharmacist	psychologist
veterinarian	economist
dentist	personnel manager
nutritionist	

People with Average Satisfaction Were

physician	high school teacher
airline pilot	funeral director
lawyer	police officer
fashion designer	clergy member
financial planner	management consultant
architect	

Fair Satisfaction Occupations Included

film directors	pre-school teachers
travel agents	TV news reporters
nurses	social workers
hotel managers	real estate agents
advertising sales	actors and actresses

Occupations with Poor Satisfaction Included

advertising sales	journalists
paramedics	automobile sales
fast food managers	apparel sales

It is not very difficult to understand why certain occupations were rated high in satisfaction. Individuals in these occupations have a great deal of control over their work style and pace. Individuals at the bottom of the list have little control over their lives (e.g. fast food manager, real estate agent, journalist) a great deal of pressure and lower pay. If work is not going well, often they feel a great deal of frustration in their entire life, with little time to work on personal or social issues.

EMERGING OCCUPATIONS

The following occupations have both excellent employment growth for the next several years, control over the work day and opportunities for success outside of the work.

- **Biotech Sales**—Biotech companies continuously develop new drugs from natural sources that are more effective than synthetic ones. More new products were approved last year than in the industry's history.

- **Cross Cultural Trainer**—As our society continues to become more diverse, the need will increase for individuals to help us fully develop and support our diversity. All areas of our society including education, business and industry and the arts will increase their demand for this training.

- **Financial Planner**—With more and more individuals becoming self employed or employed without benefits, financial planners will be needed to ensure their security.

- **Employment Attorney**—As state and federal employment laws become more complex, employment attorneys and individuals skilled in dispute resolution will be needed to handle cases ranging from age discrimination to sexual harassment.

- **Environmental Engineer**—With environmental regulations and cleanup projects increasing, government agencies and private consulting firms are looking for individuals for these positions. Universities are producing only one-third of the graduates needed for these positions.

- **Health Architect**—Continued growth in health care facilities will cause architects with health design specialization be in high demand.

- **Home Health Care Specialist**—It is predicted that employment in the home health care field will double by the year 2005. A master's degree in nursing, public health or social work, or education as a physician assistant, is preferred for home health care.

- **Industrial Hygienist**—As health problems in manufacturing increase, industrial hygienists are being hired to prevent injuries and problems.

- **Information Systems Specialist**—Developing the systems necessary to maintain records and provide information to upper level management will increase over the next two decades.

- **Local Area Network Administrator**—Local area networks are expanding at a rapid pace as mainframe computer use declines. Skilled computer analysts are needed to maintain the communication links between computers, printers, databases and workstations.

- **Physician Assistants**—Seven positions are currently available for each physician assistant. This is due to state law changes which allow PA's to conduct physical exams, order laboratory tests and dispense medicine. Home health care needs also increase opportunities.

- **Private Investigators**—As more companies, law firms and individuals seek information on others, private investigators are increasingly sought after. Women PI's are particularly in great demand.

- **Telecommunications Manager**—With the continued increased complexity of office work stations and cable television, telecommunications opportunities will continue to grow.

- **Computer Consultant**—More and more people will be purchasing home computers with little idea of how to work them.

Many Americans suffer from technophobia. Individuals who are good teachers, have a high level of interpersonal skills and are very knowledgeable about computer hardware and software will be in increasing demand.

HIGH AND LOW STRESS OCCUPATIONS

Over the last five years most jobs in the U.S. have increased in stress. As organizations have downsized, employees are asked to do more work with fewer resources. *The Jobs Rated Almanac* categorizes the following occupations:

Highest Stress Occupations

fire fighter	police officer
surgeon	highway patrol officer
mayor	basketball coach
air traffic controller	advertising executive
real estate agent	airline pilot
stockbroker	architect
attorney	insurance agent

Lowest Stress Occupations

pharmacist	medical records technician
librarian	actuary
florist	dietician
barber	cook
dental hygienist	jeweler
chemist	biologist
employment counselor	audiologist

If you want the opportunity for success both in and outside of your work, it is wise to select a lower stress occupation.

LESS WELL KNOWN OCCUPATIONS

The U.S. Department of Labor states that there are over 13,000 occupations in our country, yet most people can name fewer than fifty. How many of the following occupations did you know existed?

- **Forest Engineer**—Lays out and directs construction, installation and use of equipment in timber areas.

- **Scout**—Collects information concerning oil well drilling operations and geophysical prospecting.

- **Perfumer**—Evaluates odors and sets production standards for perfumes.

- **Geodesist**—Studies size, shape and gravitational field of the earth.

- **Philologist**—Studies structure and development of languages.

- **Immunohematologist**—Performs blood tests and consults with blood bank community.

- **Tumor Registrar**—Maintains records of hospital patients treated for cancer.

- **Sulky Driver**—Drives horse drawn two-wheel sulky in harness race.

- **Laserist**—Uses laser projectors for design and effects for entertainment of audiences.

- **Admeasurer.**—Compiles data and prepares certificates of admeasurement documents for ships.

- **Factor**—Purchases at discount accounts receivable from businesses needing operating capital.

- **Demurrage Clerk**—Compiles shipping charges and documents.

- **Mail Censor**—Opens and inspects incoming and outgoing packages to ensure compliance with prison security rules.

- **Top Screw**—Supervises and coordinates activities of cowpunchers riding after cattle on an open range.

- **Smoke Jumper**—Parachutes from airplane into forest inaccessible by ground to suppress forest fires.

- **Dip Plater**—Operates hot dip tinning machines to tinplate black pickled steel sheets.

- **Dust-Collector Operator**—Operates battery of electrical precipitators to collect metallic dust particles from fumes of smelting ore.

- **Leacher**—Controls equipment to leach out metal from ore in solution.

- **Mud Boss**—Tends machines that drain, filter, dry, crush, and package slime from electrolytic tanks to recover valuable metals such as gold and silver.

- **Maturity Checker**—Tends machines that mash peas to ascertain hardness and maturity.

- **Crutcher**—Tends machines that mix liquid, powder and paste for soap products.

- **Snailer**—Tends machines that polish watch crown and ratchet wheels.

- **Roll Reclaimer**—Tends machines that reprocess rolls of toilet tissue that do not conform to specifications.

- **Card Decorator**—Tends machines that automatically glue decorative sparkle dust to greeting cards.

- **Bucket Chucker**—Operates machines that smooth inside surface of bucket.

WHAT ARE THE NEEDS FOR NEW OCCUPATIONS

Upon reviewing the needs and concerns in our society, many new occupations can be predicted. Among the needs that are emerging in the next five years are:

- **Time Consultants**—Help deal with increasing demands and "shrinking" amount of time.

- **Home Computer Consultants**—Assist the generations who did not grow up with computers.

- **Elderly Exercise Consultants**—Will help individuals maintain their physical activity. These consultants will visit the elderly and design programs based upon their individual health and stamina.

- **Information Specialists**—There is a massive amount of information available in our society but accessing it can be a problem. Information finders, similar to the White House Boiler Room, will be developed in most cities.

- **Cable T.V. Programmers and Writers**—With hundreds of channels available on cable T.V. there is an ever increasing need for quality programs.

- **Couples Communication Counselors**—As two career families continue to expand, divorces will continue to increase. Communications counselors, at less cost than traditional psychologists, will be available to help couples develop these skills.

- **VCR Consultants**—Most Americans cannot program their VCRs. Consultants will come to your home to train people with this technology.

- **Exterior Designers**—Exterior art work in the U.S. compared to other countries is greatly lacking. Exterior designers will develop art work for bridges, buildings, roads, homes, canals, etc.

- **Stress Reduction Counselors**—In this ever demanding and complex society, Americans are feeling stress as never before. Stress reduction counselors will visit homes or offices to help people develop relaxation skills.

- **Tutors/Child Care Workers**. As education becomes more complex, the drop out rate continues to climb. Parents have little time or expertise to teach their children. Professional tutors will play a variety of roles with school aged children.

- **Crime Prevention Workers**—Our society is becoming engulfed with youth violence. Individuals are needed to work with youth as mentors and help with the difficult transitions to adulthood.

OTHER EVOLVING WORK AREAS

- medical advisor
- aquaculturalist
- cyrogenic technologist
- exotic welder
- free lance librarian
- image consultant
- marine technologist
- robot psychologist
- thesaurus designer
- color consultant
- fire fighting robot technologist

VANISHING OCCUPATIONS

As corporate budgets get tighter and computers become more sophisticated, occupations will diminish over the next ten years. Diminishing occupations include:

- **Middle Level Managers**—More responsibility will be given to upper level managers and rank and file professionals.

- **Postal Workers**—As electronic mail becomes available at home, the need for postal workers will decline.

- **Telephone Operators**—Phone companies have automated all but the most complex procedures.

- **Librarians**—Many cities and towns cannot afford to maintain libraries and most books will be available via computer.

- **Bank Tellers**—Automatic teller machines will cause a decrease in needs for these jobs.

- **Airline Attendants**—Airline budgets will mandate that these positions be cut, particularly on short flights.

Additional Resources

Excellent resources exist to provide current information on most occupations. These resources can be found in public libraries, colleges and commercial bookstores. Among the recommended publications are the following:

America's Top 300 Jobs. JIST Works, Inc., 1992.

Careers for Book Worms and Other Literary Types. M. Eberts and M. Gisle. VGM Career Horizons, 1991.

Careers for Culture Lovers and Other Artsy Types. M. Eberts and M. Gisle. VGM Career Horizons, 1992.

Careers for People Who Love to Travel. Joy Mullett and Lois Darley. Arco/Prentice Hall, 1986.

Creative Careers. Gary Blake and Robert W. Bly. John Wiley & Sons, 1985.

Dictionary of Occupational Titles. U.S. Department of Labor, 1991.

Freelance Forever. Marietta Whittlesey. Avon Books, 1982.

Green at Work. Susan Cohen. Island Press, 1992.

Jobs for English Majors and Other Smart People. John Munschauer. Peterson's Guides, 1991.

Jobs for Travel Buffs and Other Restless Types. Paul Plawin. VGM Career Horizons, 1991.

Occupational Outlook Handbook. U.S. Department of Labor, Bureau of Labor Statistics, 1994.

Offbeat Careers. The Dictionary of Unusual Work. Al Sacharov. Ten Speed Press, 1988.

The Jobs Rated Almanac. Les Krantz. Pharos Book, 1992.

12

BEST ORGANIZATIONS FOR SUCCESS

*A*t this point in your life you may have had the opportunity to work for several organizations and have likely discovered vast differences. Some organizations are very supportive of their employees' development, while others ask a lot but give little. Successful individuals seek organizations that support personal growth, either directly or indirectly. You may be considering a career change but only need to change employer. Take the same job and move it to a different company or city and you may feel completely different.

Ask the following questions of employers under consideration.

1. **Is the organization financially sound?** If you find companies are having financial problems, chances are diminished that they support employees' development. In fact they may be requesting a great deal of unpaid overtime due to inadequate funding for staffing.

2. **What is the turnover rate within the organization?** High turnover rate is a sign of dissatisfaction. If more than 30% of the employees leave every year, particularly in this tight economy, there is a problem within the organization. There

may be many reasons that contribute to the high turnover rate, but lack of support for employees is at the top of the list.

3. **Are the employees content?** What do the employees say about the organization? What do they like best and least? Employees who are treated well and receive good benefits are happy regardless of demands for hard work placed on them.

4. **Are the managers satisfied?** Dissatisfied managers can make work very uncomfortable. Are unreasonable demands placed on managers such as unreachable monthly quotas? Do they have the necessary resources to do the job? Are they experienced in handling people and problems?

5. **Is volunteering encouraged in the organization?** Does the organization care about others or only itself? If volunteering is encouraged it is a sign of a more humanistic outlook which usually carries over to employees.

6. **Are employees given a high amount of freedom to do their job?** Everyone needs to be given the flexibility to be creative and have a sense of ownership of their work. When employees are "over managed" morale tends to drop and they begin to behave like adolescents.

7. **Do high quality recreational facilities exist?** Recreational facilities allow employees to gain control of their stress. Companies that do not support recreation are in effect saying that they are not very concerned about the emotional and physical health of their staff.

8. **What is the work environment like?** Is office space cluttered or neat? Do people appear friendly or rushed? Does the work area appear congested? Are there nearby windows and fresh air? Is the furniture and equipment new or old?

9. **What provisions are made for child care?** On site child care is becoming more common. Caring employers provide child care subsidies, generous leaves for childbirth, paid leaves for new fathers, and adoption aid. Among the most supportive corporations in terms of family leave and child care are Aetna

Life and Casualty, Corning, IBM, Johnson & Johnson, and Merck & Company. On-site schools are provided by some companies, while others bring in school counselors every two months so parents can understand their children's educational progress. Other companies have on-site laundries and children's clothing swap centers.

10. **Are flexible work schedules supported?** Working at home, job sharing and compressed workweeks are increasing in organizations. People need time to complete personal and family matters.

11. **Is continued training valued and supported?** In order to do our jobs well, it is necessary to receive the latest training on computers, time management, communication skills, teamwork, supervising staff, etc. . . How often do people attend workshops, seminars and conferences? How active is the company training and development office? Are tuition stipends offered for college courses? Some organizations offer a mentoring program to allow expert employees to spread their knowledge. Other companies offer an apprenticeship program that pays workers to observe trained employees in other departments. Still other companies have extensive five to six week training programs that cover both technical knowledge and interpersonal skills.

12. **Who makes the important decisions?** Are employees involved in decision making? Is upper level management making the important decisions and leaving the time and date for the company picnic up to the other employees? What policies and procedures have changed in the last few years and have employees benefitted?

13. **Is there a family feeling and real camaraderie in the organization?** Do people support or compete with each other? Are social events occurring frequently? Do people help each other during difficult times?

14. **Are outside interests encouraged?** Some companies will have arts and crafts showings for their creative employees.

Other companies hand out running shoes for employees who walk to work. Others encourage employee participation in social action causes.

15. **Is career advancement within and outside the organization promoted?** Do they hire "home grown" managers or go outside to look for "superstars." Some companies map out a 5-10 year plan within the organization for new employees. Other organizations offer a parallel track career path for employees who do not want to move into management. Rotation of management projects so that employees can learn leadership skills is common within many progressive organizations.

After reviewing these questions give each of the company factors a rating of 1-5 in importance for you. For example if child care is extremely important rate it a five. If social events are moderately important rate it a three. If recreational facilities are not important rate it a one. After you have rated these fifteen factors, categorize them as very important, moderately important and not important at all. Then compare the organizations of interest with the important factors in a decision making grid. Your goal is to find organizations that meet as many as possible of your extremely important criteria.

	Company A	Company B	Company C	Company D
Financially sound organization				
Nice work environment				
Child care				
Flexible work schedule				
Training available				
Content employees				

CORPORATE CULTURES

Several types of organizational cultures exist in the U.S. The Venture Oriented Culture is the most demanding of all business cultures with a high burnout rate of employees. Organizations within this culture include advertising, sales, publishing, venture capitol, entertainment and management consulting. Younger employees are usually found in these companies. To be successful in this culture, employees need to be independent, decisive, adventuresome, determined, direct, efficient and competitive.

Promotion oriented companies provide fast feedback but low risk since all the chips rarely ride on one transaction. Demands are high in this culture and employees who are positive thinking, optimistic and self-motivating prosper. Organizations within this group include high tech industries, computer software and most types of sales. Successful people in this culture are gregarious, convincing, expressive, inspiring, charming, creative and energetic.

Hierarchy oriented cultures are composed of large organizations that have been around for years. People who prosper in these organizations are patient, loyal, supportive, trusting, sensitive, and considerate.

Process oriented cultures are driven by policies, rules, and regulations. Change is slow and the process is more important than outcome. When change occurs, it is usually forced from the outside. Government, banking, education, insurance and accounting are prevalent in these cultures. To be successful in this culture an employee needs to be accurate, analytical, serious, orderly, disciplined, reliable, and enjoy meetings.

In which of these corporate cultures would you feel most comfortable? Can you rank them from most desirable to least appealing? Which ones do you think would provide you the most opportunity for your success both on and off the job?

Finding Information About Organizations

Fortunately we live in an information rich society; therefore researching organizations is relatively easy. Some suggested methods to use are the following:

- Write or call a company and ask them to send you information. Most companies are willing to do this.

- Pretend you are a customer, or actually become one, and see how well they respond to your needs. If employees are not being treated well, they pass this service attitude to clients.

- Go visit an organization and/or do an informational interview. Visiting an office can give a view of the intangibles such as work environment. Talking to people who work there will give you a sense of employee satisfaction. Ask friends to recommend people to visit.

- Read printed information about an organization. Local newspapers and magazines have a great deal of information about organizations in your area. Investigate the local library for back issues of newspapers and magazines or a clippings on employers.

- Use computerized sources for national employer information. Many college libraries have excellent computerized data bases on employers. Lexus-Nexus and Compact Disclosure are national employer data banks that are updated quarterly. Info Track lists employer articles that have appeared in national newspapers and magazines.

- Take a college course that requires a paper and conduct research on employers of interest. Students often are given information unavailable to others.

Several excellent publications exist to provide information about potential organizations. *Companies That Care* describes 124 organizations that provide outstanding child-care support programs, elder-care support, time off for family matters, flexible work schedules, family support systems, and management sensitivity to family issues. At the top of their list are the following companies:

AT&T	Alley's General Store
BE&K. Inc.	Dunning, Forman, Kirrane &
Fel-Pro, Inc.	Terry
Grieco Bros., Inc.	IBM
Johnson & Johnson	S.C. Johnson & Son, Inc.
Joy Cone Co.	The Little Tikes Company
Lost Arrow Corp.	NCNB Corporation

SAS Institute Inc.   The Stride Rite Corp.
U.S. Hosiery Corp.

The 150 Best Companies for Liberal Arts Graduates provides very useful information on organizations that seek out Liberal Arts students to hire, train and promote. Some of their top companies include:

Aetna Life and Casualty   Armstrong World
Arthur Anderson   Burlington Industries
Electronic Data Systems   First Union Corp.
Goldman, Sachs & Co.   J.C. Penny
Lazarus Department Stores   May Department Stores
Scott Paper Company   T. J. Maxx
Walgreens   John Wiley & Sons

The 100 Best Companies to Work for in America includes some excellent information in the following categories:

Best for Job Security

BE&K   Ben & Jerry's Homemade
Beth Israel Hosp.,Boston   Chaparral Steel
Compaq Computer   Cooper Tire

Companies With On Site Child Care

Fel-Pro   H. B. Fuller
General Mills   Goldman Sachs
W.L. Gore & Associates

Companies With Significant Employee Ownership

Hallmark Cards   Haworth
Hershey Foods   Hewitt Assoc.

Best for Pay and Benefits

Johnson & Johnson   SC Johnson Wax
Kellog   Knight-Rider
Lands' End   Lincoln Electric

Best for Women

Motorola
Nordstrom
Odetics

Nissan Motor
Northwestern Mutual Life
Patagonia

Best Training Programs

J.C. Penney
Pitney Bowes
Preston Trucking

Physio-Control
Polaroid

Best for Minorities

Proctor & Gamble
Quad/Graphics
REI
SAS Institute
Southwest Airlines

Publix Super Markets
Reader's Digest
Rosenbluth International
J.M. Smucker

Where Fun Is a Way of Life

Springfield ReMfg.
Steelcase
Tandem
Tennant

Springs
Syntex
TDIndustries

Companies With Vacation Spots for Employees

UNUM
US West
Viking Freight System
Wegmans
Worthington Industries

USAA
Valassis Communications
Wal-Mart
Weyerhaeuser

Complete details on these companies are available within these excellent publications.

Inc. Magazine, in its July 1993 edition, provided information on the best small companies to work for in America. Their categories include the following:

Best Work and Life (outside of work):

G.T. Water Products, MoorPark, CA
Hemmings Motor News, Bennington, VT
Lancaster Laboratories, Lancaster, PA
Ridgeview Hosiery, Newton, N.C.
White Dog Enterprises, Philadelphia, PA
Wilton Connor Packaging, Charlotte, N.C.

Career Advancement

Creative Staffing, Miami, FL
Fitcorp, Boston, MA
Ideo Product Development, Palo Alto, CA
Phoenix Textile, St. Louis, MO
Prospect Associates, Rockville, MD
Stonyfield Farm, Londonderry, N.H.

Job Autonomy

Action Industries, San Diego, CA
Advanced Network Design, La Mirada, CA
Alphatronix, Research Triangle Park, N.C.
Avid Technology, Tewksbury, MA
Childress Buick, Phoenix, AZ
Job Boss Software, Minneapolis, MN

Training

Datatec Industries, Fairfield, N.J.
Dettmers Industry, Stuart, FL
Luttink Manufacturing, Menonee Falls, WI
Northwestern Tool and Die Mfg., Chicago
Starbucks Coffee, Seattle
Triton Industries, Chicago

Compensation

Ashton Photo, Salem, OR
Aspect Telecommunications, San Jose, CA
Calvert Group, Bethesda, MD

ESP Software Services, Minneapolis
Phelps County Bank, Rolla, MO
Rogan, Northbrook, IL

Love of Product

Comprehensive Rehabilitation Center, Edina, MN
Giro Sport Design, Soquel, CA
Great Plains Software, Fargo, N.D.
Manco, Westlake, OH
Odwalla, Davenport, CA
Zymol Enterprises, North Branford, CT

Additional Resources

America's Fastest Growing Employers. Carter Smith. Bob Adams Books, 1992.

Companies That Care. Hal Morgan and Kerry Tucker. Simon & Schuster, 1991.

150 Best Companies for Liberal Arts Graduates. Cheryl Woodruff and Greg Ptacek. John Wiley & Sons, 1992.

The Hundred Best Companies to Work for in America. Robert Levering and Milton Moskowitz. Doubleday, 1993.

Inc. The Magazine for Growing Companies. Boston, MA

13

SUCCESS ORIENTED PLACES TO LIVE

*H*ave you ever walked along the beach in Maui at night, felt the cool breezes and dreamed of living there? Have you ever felt the warm sun in Telluride during the summer and hiked in the spectacular mountains? How often have you sailed in the San Francisco Bay or seen the glorious fall colors in Vermont. If you are finding satisfying employment elusive, why not take this opportunity and move somewhere you have always wanted to live. Moving to a cherished location can often bring new energy and inspiration into your life. This phenomenon is most easily seen with professional athletes who get traded to a different city and perform better than ever before in their career. Besides, it's better to be unemployed somewhere you want to live, than without satisfying work in an undesirable location. Where have you always wanted to live, but could not because of your job? Aspen, Monterey, Seattle, New Orleans, Boston, Atlanta, Santa Barbara? Visit that area and try to get a sense of what it would be like to live there. Apply for jobs while there and you may be able to deduct some expenses from your taxes. Amazingly, new locations push us to be more sociable, learn quicker, and see things in a different way.

Discovering a location where you can develop your natural talents is one of the major keys to success. All cities and states do not promote the same type of accomplishments. For example larger cities promote more artistic development than smaller ones. There are more artists in San Francisco than the entire state of Wyoming. College towns promote intellectual activities. The western United States, with huge land expanses, will challenge your physical abilities. Northeastern parts of our country, with heavy population centers promote social interaction. Other factors to consider are employment opportunities, taxes, schools, health care, crime rates, and cost of living. In general it is more expensive to live on the east and west coasts, therefore people work harder to survive. In areas where it is less expensive and crime rates are lower (e.g. the western U.S.), people tend to spend less time working. Several excellent publications exist and can provide you with this information including *Life in America's Small Cities, Places Rated Almanac, The Greener Pastures Relocation Guide,* and *Country Careers*. Additionally, Chambers of Commerce in most cities and states will eagerly send you information.

Review chapter two and remind yourself of your priorities for success during the next three years. Study the cities described below to see how they might fit your needs.

INTELLECTUALLY STIMULATING CITIES

Boston, Massachusetts is the "Athens" of the United States with fifty-four colleges and universities. Lectures, seminars, and discussions on almost every issue or topic are frequently held. Adults can enroll in hundreds of classes to continue their intellectual growth. You will not be bored in Boston.

Washington, D.C. contains hundreds of museums and galleries along with many quality higher education institutions. Also, Washington is the most international city in the United States with a wide array of cultural activities.

San Francisco/Berkeley, California has twenty-five colleges and universities to maintain your intellectual stimulation. Many world class scholars live in this area and public seminars and discussions are abundant. Radio and T.V. stations present hundreds of programs on a variety of topics to keep you intellectually stimulated.

Raleigh-Durham, North Carolina, with thirteen colleges and universities is one of the intellectual centers of the south. North Carolina and Duke are two of the outstanding universities in the United States. Although not a "Boston" this area provides a great deal of intellectual activity.

Other Intellectually Stimulating Cities

New York
Los Angeles
Chicago
Baltimore
Madison, Wisconsin
Ithaca, New York
East Lansing, Minnesota
Austin, Texas

Houston
Cleveland
Ames, Iowa
Philadelphia
Berkeley, California
Minneapolis, Minnesota
Champaign-Urbana, Illinois

ARTISTIC AND CULTURAL CENTERS

New York with forty-nine art museums, twenty-six symphonies, thirty-three theaters, and twenty-seven dance companies is the number one artistic and cultural center in the United States. New York is an excellent place to start pursuing your artistic and cultural interests. Artistic work experiences in New York give excellent credentials for moving to other cities.

If New York is number one, Los Angeles is not far behind with twenty symphonies, and numerous opera companies, dance groups and theaters. Los Angeles also has many film companies and opportunities to learn about that industry.

Chicago is an outstanding cultural city with many excellent art galleries, twelve symphonies, and nine professional theaters.

Washington, D.C. ranks high in cultural activities because of its performing arts centers, museums, and international population.

San Francisco has many excellent theaters, museums, and musical talent.

Other Cultural Areas

Santa Fe, New Mexico
Boston, Massachusetts
Seattle, Washington
Cleveland, Ohio
Portland, Oregon
New Orleans, Louisiana
Portland, Maine

Rochester, New York
San Diego, California
Philadelphia, Pennsylvania
Baltimore, Maryland
Pittsburgh, Pennsylvania
Providence, Rhode Island
Nashville, Tennessee

Minneapolis, Minnesota   Rochester, Minnesota
Houston, Texas

OUTDOOR AND RECREATIONAL AREAS

Whether you prefer to work or play outdoors, the following locations will have appeal. Denver, Colorado is an outdoor lover's paradise. Close proximity to the mountains allows easy year round access to skiing, hiking, mountain biking, camping, back packing and stream fishing. Additionally, many beautiful national parks are within a few hours driving distance including Arches, Canyonlands, Rocky Mountain, and Mesa Verde.

Monterey, California and surrounding Seaside provide some of the most spectacular costal land in the United States. Sailing, fishing, golf, hiking and biking can be enjoyed year round.

Charleston and Hilton Head South Carolina is a beautiful counterpart to California without the crowds and expenses. This relatively unknown area provides wonderful sailing, golfing, biking, water skiing and beautiful beaches. Charleston itself is one of the most charming cities in the United States with multiple historical treasures.

Sarasota, Florida provides the outdoor enthusiast with abundant sailing, power boating, water skiing, biking, fishing, snorkeling, and numerous other water sports Moab, Utah has some of the most spectacular rock formations in the world. Arches and Canyonlands National Parks provide outstanding hiking, camping, four wheel driving, and biking. The Colorado River which flows through Moab provides endless fishing, canoeing and rafting.

Eugene, Oregon has over 1.4 million acres of parks and forests in addition to a beautiful coastline. Here you can find excellent water sports and outstanding camping and hiking. Some of the best recreational parks in America are located here.

Other Recreational Areas

Key West, Florida   Santa Barbara
Western Washington   Norfolk
Galveston, Texas   Savannah
New Orleans   Colorado Springs
Salt Lake City   Flagstaff
Bozeman, Montana   Newport, Rhode Island
San Luis Obispo   Corvallis, Oregon

Ames, Iowa
Brunswick, Georgia
Salt Lake City

Port Angeles, Washington
Seattle
San Diego

HIGHLY SOCIAL PLACES TO LIVE

Many cities in the United States claim to be the friendliest. This of course greatly depends on how close your culture and values fit with the residents of that area. Friendliness is also influenced by crime rates, employment opportunities and recreational activities.

Listed below are some of the places in the United States that are considered friendly:

Grand Forks, North Dakota
Rochester, Minnesota
Provo, Utah
Charleston, West Virginia
Pittsburgh, Pennsylvania
Knoxville, Tennessee
Ashville, North Carolina
Denver, Colorado
Fort Collins, Colorado
Provo, Utah
Pullman, Washington

Canton, Ohio
Bloomington, Illinois
Madison, Wisconsin
Iowa City, Iowa
Cincinnati, Ohio
Columbia, Missouri
Lincoln, Nebraska
Danbury, Connecticut
Fort Walton Beach, Florida
St. Cloud, Minnesota
Myrtle Beach, South Carolina

PLACES TO MAKE MONEY AND FIND WORK

Where are some of the places with the best chance to make money and find employment? Fastest growing states in the United States according to the Kemper Statewide Economic Indicators Analysis, Summer, 1993 include the following:

Colorado
Alaska
Wyoming
Florida
Arizona

New Mexico
North Carolina
Kentucky
New Hampshire

States with the weakest economies included:

California	Missouri
Hawaii	New York
New Jersey	Maryland
Nebraska	

Some of the cities that are projected to provide good employment opportunities include:

Washington, D.C.	Minneapolis-St. Paul
Denver	Atlanta
Seattle	Charlotte
Chicago	Raleigh-Durham
Austin	Phoenix
Pittsburgh	Nashville
Tampa-St. Petersburg	San Antonio
Las Vegas	Houston
Sioux Falls	Madison
Orlando	New Haven
Ft. Worth	Columbia
Dallas	Hartford
Wichita	Omaha
Kansas City	Tucson
Albuquerque	Salt Lake

In addition to growth, cost of living should take a high consideration unless you like working two or three jobs. Some of the areas with high cost of living are:

Stamford, Connecticut	Oakland, California
San Francisco, California	Monterey, California
Honolulu, Hawaii	Boston, Massachusetts
Los Angeles, California	Providence, Rhode Island
New York, New York	Anchorage, Alaska
Fairfax, Virginia	Somerset, New Jersey
Morris, New Jersey	Montgomery, Maryland
San Diego	Washington, D.C.
Seattle	

On the other hand, some of the most desirable areas with a lower cost of living include:

Salem, Oregon
Greeley, Colorado
Spokane, Washington
Biloxi, Mississippi
Daytona Beach, Florida
Panama City, Florida
Charleston, South Carolina
Phoenix, Arizona
Atlanta, Georgia
New Orleans, Louisiana
Knoxville, Tennessee
Salt Lake City, Utah

South Bend, Indiana
Vancouver, Washington
Chattanooga, Tennessee
Colorado Springs, Colorado
San Antonio, Texas
Savannah, Georgia
Rapid City, South Dakota
Orlando, Florida
Louisville, Kentucky
Columbia, Missouri
San Antonio, Texas

The National Association of Home Builders recently rated housing affordability and found the most expensive areas to be:

San Francisco
Los Angeles
Santa Rosa

Santa Cruz
Monterey

The least expensive areas were:

Jackson, Michigan
Brazoria, Texas
Mansfield, Ohio
Lansing, Michigan

Rockford, Illinois
Elkhand, Indiana
Milwaukee, Wisconsin
Springfield, Illinois

U.S. News and World Report recently surveyed salaries across the nation and found that they can vary widely from one region to the next. In general, the West Coast pays significantly more than any other region except for occupations such as accountants, credit representatives, human resource generalists, electricians, nurses and social workers.

Some of the best kept secrets about desirable places to live include:

Friday Harbor, Washington
Roche Harbor, Washington
Upper Peninsula of Michigan

Sun Valley, Idaho
Missoula, Montana
Crested Butte, Colorado

Sarasota, Florida   Fort Myers, Florida
Padre Island, Texas

OVERSEAS CITIES

Americans frequently overlook foreign cities as places for success. Living abroad can be a tremendous learning and growth experience and provide many opportunities. Listed below are resources with information on working and living abroad.

How to Get a Job in Europe

International Jobs: Where They Are and How to Get Them

Looking for Employment in Foreign Countries

101 Ways to Find an Overseas Job

MYERS-BRIGGS TYPOLOGY AND GEOGRAPHICAL LOCATIONS

Almost forty million Americans have taken the Myers-Briggs personality inventory for use in career decisions, personal therapy, marriage counseling and management development. This information can also be very useful in making decisions on where to live. The Myers-Briggs defines four dimensions which are:

Extrovert	**Introvert**
Prefer to be with people and active	Prefer to focus on their inner world
Sensing	**Intuitive**
Likes realities and concrete information	Prefers to use imagination and intuition

Thinking

Makes decisions based on facts and objectivity

Feeling

Makes decisions based on feelings of self and others

Judging

Likes closure, order and decisions

Perceivers

Prefer to keep option open and flexible

Myers-Briggs Types and Locations

Extroverts

East Coast such as New York, Boston, Philadelphia Midwest: Chicago.

Introverts

New Hampshire, Maine, Wyoming, Utah, North Dakota, New Mexico

Sensors

Pittsburgh, Philadelphia, Wisconsin, Michigan, Minnesota, Washington, Colorado, Indiana, Alaska, Ohio

Intuitives

Santa Fe, Berkeley, Nashville, Las Vegas, New York, San Francisco

Thinkers

Washington, D.C., Princeton, New Jersey, Berkeley, Palo Alto, Cambridge, Boston

Feelers

North Carolina, South Carolina, Arkansas, Texas

Judgers

Midwest, Texas, Los Angeles, Maine, Vermont, New Hampshire, Massachusetts, Colorado Springs, Sacramento

Perceivers

Santa Barbara, Boulder, San Francisco, Newport Beach, Sedona, Arizona, New Orleans, Sarasota, Virginia

DECIDING ON YOUR BEST SUCCESS CITY

If you have more than three appealing locations under consideration, try to narrow the choices. Once again, it is helpful to use a logical process inherent in the decision making grid. First, list all of the locations that you are considering in a column down the left side of a piece of paper. Next, across the top of the page list all of the factors that are important to you. Now, in the intersecting blocks write a yes, no, or ?. Then add the yeses and prioritize your options.

	Recreation	Jobs	Culture	Friendly	Warm
Boise	yes	?	no	yes	no
Chicago	no	?	yes	?	no
Denver	yes	yes	?	yes	no
Corvallis	yes	no	no	yes	?
San Diego	yes	yes	yes	?	yes
Atlanta	?	yes	?	yes	yes
Santa Fe	yes	no	yes	?	yes

You can see from this list that Denver, San Diego, Atlanta and Santa Fe are the highest rated based upon the expressed needs. After determining the top three places to live, try to visit the locations and get a real life feel for them. During your visit, you should be assessing:

1. Friendliness of the residents
2. Availability of housing
3. Ease of getting around
4. Climate
5. Networking opportunities
6. How well your career and life style can be met there
7. Employment opportunities
8. Cost of living

My Ideal Locations   **Reasons**

1._____   _____
2._____   _____
3._____   _____

Happy Journeys!

Additional Resources

Country Careers. Jerry Germer. Audio Tech Business Book Services, 1993.

How to Get a Job in Europe. Robert Sanborn, Surrey Books, 1993.

International Jobs. Where They Are: How to Get Them. Eric Kocher. Addison-Wesley Publishing Co., 1989.

Life in America's Small Cities. G. Scott Thomas Prometheus Books, 1990.

Looking for Employment in Foreign Countries. June Aulick. World Trade Academy Press, Inc., 1990.

Places Rated Almanac. R. Boyer and D. Savageau. Prentice Hall, 1989.

The Greener Pastures Relocation Guide. Alfred Shattuck. Prentice Hall, 1984.

Type Talk. Otto Kroeger and Janet Thuesen. Delta Books, 1988.

101 Ways to Find an Overseas Job. Francine Modderno Cantrell Corporation, 1987.

14

OWNING YOUR OWN BUSINESS AND TEMPORARY WORK

When an individual's self esteem rises, the desire to be self-employed goes up. Motivation to start a new business may come from being laid off from an organization, feeling that a spin off company could be successful, or a desire to begin something new of one's own.

Neil Johnson was a engineering manager for a major aerospace company. A few years ago he was making over $100,000 managing the planning division. When downsizing occurred, Neil accepted an early retirement package. Two years later, Neil is the owner of a print shop and is approaching his previous salary.

Richard Emerson was head of the English Department at Wade High School in Oklahoma City. His salary was not enough to support his family so Richard started a construction company. Most of his construction experience came while working summers with his uncle.

Mary Rowe was a human resources manager with a women's clothing manufacturer. After several years of feeling she was not needed, Mary is now finding great enjoyment as owner of a small clothing store.

Fred Baldwin was laid off after twelve years in the computer business. Recently Fred purchased a computer outlet in Washington D.C. and sells lap top and personal computers.

Sara Peterson was fired several times from previous human resources jobs because she "knew better" than her supervisors how to run the departments. Five years ago Sara started her own benefits consulting firm and now has six employees. The most rewarding part of her work is the free assistance she gives to the elderly.

YOUR OWN BUSINESS

Thousands of career changes are made yearly by people moving from working in an organization to owning their own businesses. Most professionals who leave organizations go into consulting, start up small companies, or purchase franchises. Franchises account for more than a third of all U.S. retail sales and employ nearly seven million people. The average franchise investment is $150,000 but can range from $25,000 to $500,000. Approximately 90 percent of franchises succeed compared to only 30 percent of other new businesses! The fastest growing franchises last year were automotive products and services, business services, security systems, beauty and bath products, and postal services.

HOME BUSINESS

Another rapidly growing area of small business ownership is the home business arena. Working at home has the advantage of lowered business costs and personal convenience. Also parents with small children find that home businesses can provide time for family responsibilities. Before starting a home business, it is wise to determine which businesses can prosper in a home, if there is a need for the business or service in your area, how high the start up costs will be, and how easy it is to get into the business. Also you must know what your skills are and how well they fit with the proposed business. Talk with people who have started a home business to understand the potential pitfalls and ways to overcome them.

Some of the home businesses that are projected to be profitable during the next few years include:

- Antique Buying and Selling
- Association Management
- Bed and Breakfasts
- Cleaning Services
- Computer Consultants
- Computer Trainer

- Computer Repair
- Desk Top Publishing
- Direct Marketing
- Errand Service
- Gift Baskets
- Hair Styling
- Specialty Foods Grower
- Information Search
- Mail Order Business
- Medical Transcriber
- Private Investigator
- Professional Practice Consultant
- Resume Writing Services
- Real Estate Appraiser
- Snow Removal
- Auto Decals
- Low Cost Newsletters
- Community Identity Events
- Community Tours
- Open Houses for Crafts People
- Events Tickets
- Fund Raising
- Reminder Services
- Exercise Assistants
- Technical Writer
- Word Processing Service
- Fitness Trainer
- Moving Service
- Manufacturers Agent
- In-Home Health Care
- Pet Sitter
- Sign Maker
- Social Referral Agent
- Employment Counselor
- Communication Consultant

ON THE ROAD

Opportunities for profit usually increase when individuals take their
home businesses on the road. One prevalent example is the gourmet
coffee carts that are now located in libraries, shopping malls, and other

public institutions. Another example is mobile automobile glass repairs. Where else, besides in their home or shop could the following business be located?

- Hair styling
- Shoe repairs
- Psychological counseling
- Selling tickets
- Designing clothes

FRANCHISING

Trisha Feigin was an employee benefits administrator who worked in a medium sized engineering corporation for 28 years. When the company was sold, Trisha began to look for options and found one in Fantastic Sam's hair salons. "I wanted to do something that did not involve a lot of inventory," says Trisha, who now owns two salons. Neither she nor her husband cut hair but primarily handle personnel and financial matters.

Opportunities in franchising increase every year and in 1992 alone the number of franchise establishments rose about five percent to 430,000 nationally. Success rates for franchises are very high. A recent study by Arthur Anderson & Co. found that 86 percent of all franchises were under the same ownership after five years and only three percent were no longer in business at all. In contrast, a study by the Small Business Administration reported that 62 percent of all new businesses went bust in their first six years. The cost to purchase a franchise ranges from $25,000 to $500,000. Loans are available through the U.S. Small Business Association or independent finance companies such as:

Allied Capital Corp.
1666 K St. N.W. #901
Washington, D.C. 20006
202-331-1112

ITT Small Business
Finance Corp.
2055 Craigshire Rd. #400
St. Louis, MO 63146
800-447-2025

First Western SBLC Inc.
2000 Bering Dr. #805
Houston, TX 77057
713-785-5454

Business Loan Center
777 Third Ave., 32nd Fl.
New York, NY 10017
212-751-5626

Bay Bank & Trust Co.   The Money Store
509 Harrison Ave.   Investment Corp.
Panama City, FL 32401   17530 Ventura Blvd., #206
904-769-3333   Encino, CA 91316
                                        818-906-2999

Franchises are available in the following areas:

Apparel and Accessories   Home Improvement
Automotive   Products and Services
Pet Care   Hotels and Motels
Beauty and Health   Maintenance Services
Building Products and   Photo/Video Services
  Services   Printing Services
Business Services   Publishing
Personnel Services   Real Estate
Children's Products   Recreation
  and Services   Restaurants
Education and Training   Travel
Environmental Services   Retail Food
Fast Food

For a listing of organizations that sell franchises in these areas review
Entrepreneur Magazine's Guide to Franchise and Business Opportunities,
1994 Annual Report. A new breed of entrepreneur on the market these
days is the "ultrapreneur." In his new book *Ultrapreneuring,* James
Arkebauer describes these individuals as entrepreneurs who start up
businesses, with the goal of selling them in a few years. Ultrapreneural
business plans include a clearly defined exit strategy and selling oneself
out of a job.

BEST CITIES TO START A BUSINESS

Not all cities will provide the same opportunities for small business
success. Some of the most important factors to consider when selecting
a location are:

- **General Economic Health**. If a city is facing a recession, your
  chances of success are diminished. Review *Money Magazine's*
  September, 1993 issue for the latest economic information.
  Currently some of the cities with the fastest growing economies

are Madison, Wisconsin; Sioux Falls, North Dakota; and Raleigh/Durham, North Carolina; Columbia, South Carolina; Phoenix; Salt Lake City; Albuquerque; Kansas City; Austin.

■ **Available Labor Pool.** What type of people do you need to hire, if any? Some cities have a wealth of highly trained technical people while others have many lower paid laborers.

■ **Fit Between Products and Services and People Who Live in the Location.** If you are starting a lawn care business, suburbs are better than inner cities. Ever try selling heating systems in Arizona? Good luck! Make sure you conduct a market analysis and determine whether there is a need for your business in that area.

■ **Costs of Office and Industrial Space.** There is a wide range of costs for office space throughout the U.S. Several publications can give you an idea of where the bargains are located.

■ **Business Taxes** will vary from location to location. State tax publications will give you an idea of where taxes are the lowest and highest. Nevada, Wyoming, Washington, and South Dakota, have no corporate income taxes. Connecticut, Iowa, North Dakota, Pennsylvania and Washington, D.C. have tax rates 10 percent or higher.

■ **Locating Close to Industry.** If you have a product that is being sold to industry, it best to be located in close proximity. Employers are usually more concerned about service than sales price and realize that products sold nationally may come with poor service.

SELF ASSESSMENT AND DECISION MAKING

Before purchasing a franchise or starting a home business, assess whether these are the best options for you. Most individuals who are successful in small businesses are smart, competitive, in excellent health and have a very high energy level. Take another look at your past work experiences over the last fifteen years for patterns of likes and dislikes. Do your likes show a high amount of desire for independence, decision making, being in charge, promoting and developing, and risk taking? Did they say you need variety, challenge and nontraditional work hours? If so, owning a small business may be appropriate for you. What about your dislikes? Did they show a disdain for structure, being too specialized, not having enough decision making or control over your work day, and having to process decisions with others. Was there also a dissatisfaction with lack of challenge and advancement? These are common dislikes of people in small business.

Review your accomplishments over the past ten years? Do they show a pattern of creating or developing new products and services, being in charge and making decisions? When the adolescent years of small businesses owners is reviewed, there is a lot of lawn cutting, paper delivering, craft making and other part time jobs requiring personal initiative. How about your perfect, ideal job? Whom would you be working with, where would you be working, what types of tasks would you be performing? Does this show independence, management, dealing with people and striving for accomplishment. If so, owning a small business is one of your needs.

It is also very important to assess your skills, including technical and interpersonal skills, learned through your education and work experiences? What types of small business or franchises would your skills best support? Do you have good organizational, financial and sales skills or would someone else be available to assist you in these matters?

Research the types of franchises and best small businesses to start. Resources that can be very helpful include the following:

Entrepreneur Magazine, August & September, 1993

The Source Book of Franchise Opportunities

250 Home Based Businesses

The Rating Guide to Franchises

Building a Mail Order Business

Small Business Sourcebook

The Start Up Guide: A One-Year Plan for Entrepreneurs

Chambers of Commerce have small business councils or meetings that you can attend with small business owners. Interview people who have started small businesses to discover success strategies. Try asking the following questions:

1. What do they like best and least about owning the business?
2. How much money would someone need to start a business or franchise?
3. What are some sources of loans or grants?
4. What skills are most important to be successful in the business?
5. Where can these skills be obtained?
6. How do they market their business and what assistance is available?
7. What would they do differently if they could start their business again?
8. What are some of the most profitable franchises and small businesses?
9. Where did they find professional assistance such as lawyers and accountants?
10. Whom do they have as employees? How did they find them? What are their responsibilities? What type of training did they need?
11. What type of health insurance do they have and where was it purchased?
12. How are they saving for retirement?

Next, try to get some work experience in the franchise or small business of interest. Approach several business owners and see if you can volunteer or work for minimum salary for three to six months. Draw up a contract that says you agree not to start a similar business in the same geographical location for the next ten years. Most small business owners would love to have another adult working for them if there was a non-competition guarantee. If you are a true entrepreneur, after the three to six month period, you should be eager to start your own business. Your former employer can be a consultant and may even refer clients.

THE ENTREPRENEURIAL TEST

Take the following quiz to help you determine whether starting your own business would be a good idea.

1. How were your parents employed?
   a. Both worked and were self-employed most of their working lives.
   b. Both worked and were self employed for some part of their working lives.
   c. One parent was self-employed for most of his or her working life.
   d. One parent was self-employed at some point in his or working life.

2. Have you ever been fired from a job?
   a. More than once
   b. Once
   c. Never

3. Are you an immigrant or were your parents or grandparents immigrants.
   a. I was born outside of the U.S.
   b. One or both of may parents were born outside the U.S.
   c. At least one of my grandparents were born outside the U.S.
   d. None of the above.

4. Your work career has been:
   a. Primarily in small businesses under 100 employees.
   b. Primarily in medium-sized businesses, 100-500 employees.
   c. Primarily in big businesses over 500.

5. Did you operate any businesses before you were twenty?
   a. Many
   b. A few
   c. None

6. What is your present age?
   a. 21-30
   b. 31-40
   c. 41-50
   d. Over 50

7. You are the _____ child in the family.
   a. Oldest
   b. Middle
   c. Youngest
   d. Other

8. You are:
   a. Married
   b. Divorced
   c. Single

9. Your highest level of formal education is:
   a. Some high school
   b. High school diploma
   c. Some college
   d. Bachelors degree
   e. Master's degree
   f. Doctorate or professional degree

10. What is your primary motive in starting a business?
    a. To make money
    b. Do not like working for someone else
    c. To be famous
    d. As an outlet for excess energy

11. Your relationship to the parent who provided most of the family's income was:
    a. Strained
    b. Comfortable
    c. Competitive
    d. Nonexistent

12. You find the answers to difficult questions by:
    a. Working hard
    b. Working smart
    c. Both

13. On whom do you rely for critical management advice?
    a. Internal management teams
    b. External management professionals
    c. External financial professionals
    d. No one except myself

14. If you were on the racetrack, which would you bet on?
    a. The daily double — a chance to make a killing
    b. The 10-to-1 shot
    c. A 3-to-1 shot
    d. The 2-to-1 favorite

15. The only ingredient that is both necessary and sufficient for starting a business is:
    a. Money
    b. Customers
    c. An idea or product
    d. Motivation and hard work

16. At a cocktail party, you:
    a. Are the life of the party
    b. Never know what to say to people
    c. Just fit into the crowd
    d. Never go to cocktail parties
17. You tend to "fall in love" too quickly with:
    a. New product ideas
    b. New employees
    c. New manufacturing ideas
    d. New financial plans
    e. All of the above
18. Which of the following personality types is best suited to be your right-hand person?
    a. Bright and energetic
    b. Bright and lazy
    c. Dumb and energetic
19. You accomplish tasks better because:
    a. You are always on time
    b. You are super organized
    c. You keep good records
20. You hate to discuss:
    a. Problems involving employees
    b. Signing expense accounts
    c. New management practices
    d. The future of the business
21. Given a choice, you would prefer:
    a. Rolling dice with a 1-in-3 chance of winning
    b. Working on a problem with a 1-in-3 chance of solving it in the time allocated
22. If you could choose between the following competitive professions, your choice would be:
    a. Professional golf
    b. Sales
    c. Personal counseling
    d. Teaching
23. If you had to choose between working with a partner who is a close friend and working with a stranger who is an expert in your field, you would choose:
    a. The close friend
    b. The expert

24. In business situations that demand action, clarifying who is in charge will help produce results.
    a. Agree
    b. Agree with reservations
    c. Disagree
25. In playing a competitive game, you are concerned with:
    a. How well you play
    b. Winning or losing
    c. Both of the above
    d. Neither of the above

SCORING

Instructions: Assign the following weighted numerical scores to correspond to the letter of your answer.

1. a-10 b-5 c-5 d-2 e-0	8. a-10 b-2 c-2	14. a-0 b-2 c-10 d-3	20. a-8 b-10 c-0 d-0
2. a-10 b-7 c-0	9. a-2 b-3 c-10 d-8 e-4	15. a-0 b-10 c-0 d-0	21. a-0 b-15
3. a-5 b-4 c-3 d-0	10. a-0 b-15 c-0 d-0	16. a-0 b-10 c-3 d-0	22. a-3 b-10 c-0 d-0
4. a-10 b-5 c-0	11. a-10 b-5 c-10 d-5	17. a-5 b-5 c-5 d-5 e-15	23. a-0 b-10

5. a-10	12. a-0	18. a-2	24. a-10
b-7	b-5	b-10	b-2
c-0	c-10	c-0	c-0
6. a-8	13. a-0	19. a-5	25. a-8
b-10	b-10	b-15	b-10
c-5	c-0	c-5	c-15
d-2	d-5		d-0
7. a-15			
b-2			
c-0			
d-0			

Now add all of your scores. If you scored:

- 225-275, chances are excellent of being a successful entrepreneur.
- 190-224, chances are good you will succeed.
- 150-189, chances are borderline.
- Below 150, better stay a hired hand.

PART TIME AND TEMPORARY WORK

The traditional American job, with a 40 hour workweek, medical benefits and a pension at age 65 is rapidly disappearing. Temporary employees now make up more than half of new hires. Many companies have adopted a form of work force management to compete in the world market. They keep a core of full time managers and valued workers and add other employees as business demands. Another new approach is the leasing of employees. Under a leasing agreement, employees continue to work for their current employer, but a leasing company "hires" them, then leases back to the employer. This makes the leasing company the employer of record for tax and insurance purposes. The employer is able to hand over the paperwork to the leasing company. According to the CAM Report, the number of leased workers increased from just 10,000 in 1984 to more than 950,000 last year, and is expected to grow to a least 10 million by the mid-1990's.

Making the Most of Temporary Work

Temporary work is viewed by many people in a negative way and it does not provide the desired security, benefits or opportunities for advancement. This is a limited view of temporary work because thousands of people each year move from temporary positions to permanent employment. Additionally it is important to remember that no job is really permanent, particularly with our constantly changing employment patterns. Three to four years is the average employment with an organization and therefore we must always be thinking about our next career moves.

What are some of the potential advantages of temporary employment?

- It allows you to meet new people and make business contacts.
- Opportunities are available to learn about different organizations.
- New challenges are constantly provided.
- If you enjoy traveling, it gives you an opportunity to live in different cities or countries and still earn money.
- Opportunities to explore different career options are provided.
- You can work without the commitment of a full time job, therefore leaving time to explore outside work interests.
- It gives you more time to be with your family.
- You learn new skills and can improve your resume.
- Valuable work references can be obtained.
- Time will be available to take college courses and earn degrees.

Maximizing Your Temporary Assignment

Several keys exist to getting the most from your temporary work within an organization.

- Work within organizations where there is employment growth. This of course assumes you are interested in staying there for a longer period of time. Before accepting a position, do some research on the organization to find out how well they are doing financially and avoid ones that are going downhill.

- Some organizations are on the cutting edge. In these organizations you will have a greater opportunity to learn new skills that will make you stand out when applying in other organizations.

- Network within the organization and get to know other departments and divisions where your skills might be used. Attend after hours social events and try to make friends in other departments.

- Make a good impression with your supervisor and his/her supervisor. These people can provide valuable references and full time employment opportunities.

- Get to know key people in the Human Resources Department within the organization. These individuals are essential for finding a full time position within the organization.

- Learn as many new skills as you can. Try attending workshops and seminars to improve your abilities even if you have to make up time.

- Learn about the organization's competitors and places that may have full time positions.

Additional Resources

Building a Mail Order Business. John Wiley, 1991.

Buying and Selling a Small Business. U.S. Small Business Administration, 1978.

Entrepreneur Magazine, New York, 1993.

Small Business Sourcebook. Carol Schwartz. Gale Research, 1993.

Starting and Managing a Small Business Service. U.S. Small Business Administration, 1990.

The Rating Guide to Franchises. Dennis Foster. Facts on File, 1990.

The Source Book of Franchise Opportunities. Robert E. Bond. Dow Jones-Irwin, 1988.

The Start Up Guide: A One Year Plan for Entrepreneurs. David H. Bargs.

The Temp Worker's Handbook. William Lewis and Nancy Schuman. American Management Association, 1988.

250 Home Based Jobs. Scott Olson. Arco, 1990.

15 | EMPOWERING EMPLOYMENT SEEKING

A colleague of mine once suggested that job seekers should first do some risky physical activities before they begin looking for work. "After parachuting from an airplane or taking a three day raft trip on a turbulent river, the risks in job seeking will, by comparison, seem minor."

Believe it or not, job seeking can actually be somewhat enjoyable if you know how to play the game and have the right attitude. When else is the opportunity available to meet so many people and learn in-depth information about organizations? Why then is job seeking approached with such apprehension? Most people are very fearful of rejection and would do anything to avoid it. The reality of life is that there will be a certain amount of rejection that cannot be avoided. Ask most successful people and they will describe a great deal of rejection in their lives. Dealing positively and learning from this rejection is the true indication of future successes.

Team up with other job seekers and meet once a week to discuss rejections and success. Give the person with the most rejections an award (e.g. free lunch) for his/her effort. A high number of rejections is an indication of a good efforts and successes.

The second reason job seeking is not seen favorably is that individuals do not know the most effective ways to find employment. If you follow the standard procedures of job seeking, there is only a 25 percent chance of finding employment. Creativity and risk taking are essential elements of job seeking.

FIVE BASIC MISTAKES IN JOB SEEKING

- **Mistake #1—Not Knowing What You Want.** After a few months, job seekers may say "I'll take anything." Unfortunately, employers do not hire people for "anything," but rather to fulfill positions which require unique skills and interests. One of the first steps in job seeking is knowing the skills you can offer an employer.

- **Mistake #2—Sending Out Too Many Resumes.** Confused job seekers will often send out hundreds of resumes. After this they wait and wait. . .and wait for replies. If you are using this method to obtain work, make sure you have many hobbies and a lot of good books to read. Employers rarely respond to mass mailed resumes.

- **Mistake #3—Using Want Ads as Your Main Source of Employment.** As you may have noticed, the worst jobs are advertised in want ads. This is because employers cannot find individuals to fill these positions and therefore must market to everyone. Occasionally a naive employer lists a quality position in the want ads and becomes inundated with responses.

- **Mistake #4—Applying for Positions Through the Human Resources Department in Organizations.** Unfortunately Human Resources Departments are usually overworked, understaffed and the last to know about openings in their organization. Often, individuals have already decided who will be hired and then contact the Human Resources Department. Ask individuals who have been hired in large organizations when they learned about their position and most will admit several weeks before it was officially announced in the Human Resources Department.

- **Mistake #5—Assuming the Best Qualified Person Gets the Job.** Frequently employers will hire less qualified individuals who show a great deal of enthusiasm for the position and the organization. Do not be put off by lack of experience, if you possess good interpersonal skills, high energy and some of the skills necessary for the position.

BEFORE YOU BEGIN THE JOB SEARCH

Before initiating a job search some important preparation is necessary.

- **Team up with other people who are also job seeking.** Have you ever tried to paint a house or room by yourself? It takes a long time and is not much fun. The same is true for job seeking. Done alone it is a burden, while conducted with others is easier; it gives you an opportunity to laugh, cry, scream and share stories.

- **Get organized before starting job seeking.** Set up a schedule in which you can dedicate 20-25 hours a week, if you are unemployed and 10-15 hours if employed or in school full time. Clarify goals for each week and hours that are best for you. Dedicate time to researching potential employers, updating your resume, networking, calling employers, meeting with your job seeking friends and other related activities. During the other 40-50 waking hours participate in activities that give you feelings of success and maintain your energy level such as biking, movies, reading, traveling, socializing, gardening, etc. These activities must bring energy into your life, not drain you. Like a marathon race, you must pace yourself or burn out will occur. No one wants to hire tired, frustrated people.

- **Create an outstanding resume since it is your calling card.** Excellent publications on resume writing are available at most bookstores; therefore, the only suggestion here is to make sure that your job objective and resume mirror the position for which you are applying. Changing your resume and job objective for each position you seek is wise. Do not rely on a cover letter to sell you for a position because many employers do not read this easily altered document. A resume is a better indication of your true skills.

- **Learn high quality interviewing skills.** Why are candidates not hired solely based upon their resumes? This document supposedly contains all of the information necessary to make a decision. Obviously there is a major question that cannot be determined by resumes, mainly your personality and how you will fit within the department. Therefore it is very important to be enthusiastic, a very likeable person and your social best during the interview. Preparing for interviews includes self assessment, researching employers and preparing answers to potential questions. Review earlier chapters of this book for skills and values assessment. Information on employers can be obtained through university or public libraries or by calling an organization and asking for information. Newspapers and magazines can keep you updated with current information. Preparing answers to questions is important to avoid stumbling through interviews. Review the job announcement for duties and responsibilities and develop a list of questions you would ask to determine if the candidates had the necessary skills. Often these questions assess how you would deal with a particular situation or problem. It is helpful to outline two or three key points you would like to make for each question. Practice answering these questions with a friend or do a video practice interview. Since at least sixty percent of what an interviewer notices is non-verbal behavior, it is important to observe and improve expressions, dress, length of answers, directness of answers, enthusiasm and demeanor.

- **Learn to be Pleasantly Assertive.** Successful job seeking is grounded in pleasant assertiveness. What does this mean? You are persistent in your job seeking but are very friendly and upbeat to everyone. Passivity will get you nowhere and aggressiveness will close doors. If assertiveness is difficult for you, as it is for many people, take an assertiveness workshop. Orient the workshop to job seeking and you will obtain ideas and energy to make job seeking much easier. Sue Pate had several years experience in sales, and decided it was time to work for a new employer. After researching potential employers, four stood out among the rest. At 9 A.M. the next

Tuesday, Sue visited one employer's office and asked to speak with the sales manager. The receptionist said that the sales manager was in a meeting but she would pass her resume to him. Sue, realizing that she would be giving up her power by leaving the resume, asked the receptionist in a pleasantly assertive manner if she would request the sales manager to speak with her for two minutes and she would be on her way. Since she was pleasant and assertive and stated how much she wanted to work there, the receptionist agreed to speak with the sales manager. Upon returning, the receptionist again said that the sales manager was busy but would review her resume later that day. Sue responded that she did not have anything as important to do that day and would just wait in the reception area until the sales manager was available. After forty-five minutes in which Sue kept talking, the receptionist once again asked the sales manager to talk with Sue so she could get rid of her. They met and talked for three minutes, set up an appointment for the next day and Sue ended up with a job offer from that company. A similar strategy should be used by most job seekers. There are many qualified people seeking the "good positions" but very few who are willing to demonstrate extremely high interest in working for an employer. Extra energy can make candidates stand out among other job seekers. Frequently job seekers are not aware that the person hired had no better skills than they did but showed additional enthusiasm. Assertive strategies that have been successful include greeting the employer in the parking lot before work with coffee and pastries, finding out what projects were not completed by the person leaving the position and bringing in ideas to finish them, and talking to key employees about the organization before the interview. Remember, you have a lot of power in the job search but you have to be creative and take risks.

FOUR WAYS TO FIND EMPLOYMENT

STRATEGY 1: Network

Networking is very effective in job seeking. If used well, networking can eliminate a lot of the difficulties with finding work. Additionally, networking can be an enjoyable way to meet people, discover information about organizations and, of course, find employment. In its most basic form, networking means telling many unfamiliar people that you are looking for employment in a specific field and asking if they know of anyone who hires for that type of position. Networking can be conducted while waiting in line, at social events, with your next door neighbor or riding the bus. You can network with former employers, past co-workers, friends and relatives, sales people, consultants, doctors, dentists, and clergy. Matt Clark was waiting for the bus to go downtown and started talking to a stranger about his ideal work, writing sports stories for a newspaper. The stranger said he knew someone in that position who worked for a local newspaper and suggested that Matt go talk with that person. Matt did and ended up obtaining a half time position.

John, a lawyer, was new to town and knew no one. He was not sure how to obtain a position but one day he went to the public library and found a book that gave short biographical sketches of the attorneys in the city. John wrote down the names of all the lawyers who went to the same law school as he did (there were two), lawyers who went to small, private undergraduate colleges on the east coast (23) and lawyers who said they skied (quite a few). He then started calling those individuals to inquire about job openings and found them very receptive. One person gave John the name of six other lawyers and told him to call back for more names if he did not find work in a week. It actually took John only ten days to find a legal position in a city with many, many lawyers.

Individuals will help you find work if you tell them you are looking. Unfortunately many people are embarrassed to ask for help and therefore miss opportunities. Compile a list of fifteen people to network with in the next two weeks. Call them, set up an appointment or lunch meeting and tell them the type of position you seek to let them assist you. Another excellent place to network is within professional associations. Professional association listings can be found easily by looking under "associations" or "professional" in the local yellow pages. These organizations usually meet at least once a month for lunch, dinner and special programs. Potential members usually can attend several functions before joining. Attend a couple of events with the goal of meeting two or three members. Get to know them and discuss your background and the type of position you are seeking. Also ask for names of other professionals to contact and permission to say you were referred by them. Repeat this process three times a week and in one month you can have twenty or thirty people helping with your job search. These individuals will know about job openings that will never appear in newspapers or other printed sources. Even after acquiring a position it is wise to stay in contact with your network by sending them birthday or holiday cards, or seeing them socially. You never know when your next job search will begin.

Claudia Pederson was at a social event one Saturday night and told several strangers that she would be interviewing next week for a city planning position. One person at the party had recently left his position in that very same office and asked her if she would like to see his personal copy of the long range plans for the city. Do you think she was interested? No, she was ecstatic. The interviewing team was very impressed the following week with Claudia's knowledge and she received the job offer.

Sometimes people find jobs by accident. An automobile accident occurred outside of Ray's apartment. While waiting for the police to arrive, he started talking to a neighbor. Ray found out that the local hospital would soon be looking for an accountant. The next day he applied for the job and three weeks later was hired. Ray truly found his position by "accident."

Your existing network contains many people who can help, some of whom you may have even forgotten. Try listing people in the following categories who can help you with your job search. Also seek people who have as much in common with you as possible (e.g. gender, ethnicity, education, religion) because they will be most empathetic of your situation.

Former Employers
Past Working Associates
Friends and Relatives
Neighbors
Business Owners
Salespeople
Consultants
Bankers

Lawyers and Accountants
College Associates
Doctors and Dentists
Insurance and Real Estate Sales People
Clergy
Civic Leaders
Club Members
People with Similar Interests
People Met While Traveling

STRATEGY 2: Respond to
Job Announcements

Most employers announce job openings in newspapers, professional newsletters, magazines, hot lines, specialized bulletins and through other sources. Many of these publications can be found in public libraries, collegiate career centers, state employment agencies, and other locations. Since these sources are rather well known, competition will be high for these openings. Uncover as many sources as possible with positions that appeal to you. Spend only five to ten percent of your job search time responding to employer's announcements because only five to ten percent of quality jobs are announced in this manner.

STRATEGY 3: Go Directly to Employers

This effective way to find employment puts you in the driver's seat. Rather than waiting for employers to announce vacancies, take your candidacy to them. The steps involved in this process include the following.

- Identify twenty-five employers who hire people with your background and qualifications. State manufacturers directories, social service guides, contacts influential for your city, or even local telephone books will be helpful gathering this infor-mation. Next, obtain more in-depth information about the organization and its products, services, clientele, new projects, salary and benefits, problems and issues, and hiring trends. This information can be obtained through college libraries and career offices, public libraries, writing the organization, and talking to people employed in the organization. Use the decision making grid, to decide on the ten organizations that interest you the most and put the others on a secondary list.

- Send your resume and cover letter, specifically oriented to the organization's needs directly to the department head where you would like to work. If you cannot find the names of department heads in any printed source, just call the organization. Cover letters generally have three parts. The first short paragraph tells the reader about your desire to work in the organization and statements demonstrating your depth of knowledge about the organization will catch the reader's attention. Use positive information obtained in a recent edition of a national or local publication such as new products or services, research, expansion plans, new contracts. It is ineffective to have your first paragraph say something like "I am applying to your organization because it is a leader in the field and has outstanding products and services." They hear this frequently and pay no attention to it.

  The second paragraph should be a summary of your skills and experiences that best fit the type of position being sought in the department. This will lead the reader to more in-depth scrutiny of your resume.

  The third paragraph is the "what's next" section. Try not to say, "please contact me if you have any openings in the next twenty years." State that you will call him/her to set up an appointment at their convenience. In a few days, follow up with a phone call to the department head and request an interview. Access to the department head can be a challenge. Try to call before 8 a.m. or after 5 p.m. because the department head will often answer the phone. If you cannot bypass the secretary tell him/her that Mr./Ms. Smith is expecting your phone call. After all, you said in your letter that you would call. If you leave a message, there is a good chance no call will be returned, so find a good time to call back.

When you get the department head on the phone, there may be only one or two minutes to sell yourself, therefore, writing a script can facilitate this conversation. This script should include the type of position you are seeking, your experience and skills and your high interest in the organization. Ask to set up an appointment at their convenience. If you are told that there are no job openings, still request an interview because positions may occur in the near future. If the department head is adamant about not seeing you, thank him or her for the time and ask if other departments in the company might be hiring someone with your skills. Also ask if would be acceptable to call back in one month because you are highly interested in the organization.

Often people feel uncomfortable using this technique because they assume it is an annoyance to department heads. Usually this is not true and most good department heads are always looking for highly motivated and skilled employees. The better the employees, the more productive their department and easier their job. Additionally, department heads, not human resource departments, know when people will be fired or have given notice as well as of departmental expansion.

This is a basic marketing technique that is used very effectively in sales. Guess what happens to your resume when it is sent unsolicited to one hundred employers. On the other hand, talking with the department head in person greatly increases your chances of obtaining employment.

When approaching small companies, the strategy is slightly different. Small companies prefer job seekers to walk in off the street rather than advertising for positions and being flooded with hundreds of resumes. So, instead of mailing your resume and following up with phone calls, visit the company and ask to speak to a manager or owner about employment opportunities. Dress for an interview and bring a copy of your resume. Often you will have an immediate opportunity to talk with individuals having hiring authority and express your interest in working for that organization. Make sure that you have researched the company and tell them specifically why you are interested in working for them. On your resume and in your interview with a small company, stress a strong desire for responsibility, variety in your work, ability to work without a great deal of supervision, being a team player and enjoyment of working in a small company atmosphere. This will be music to their ears.

STRATEGY 4: Conduct Informational Interviewing

The primary purpose of informational interviewing is to obtain information and help with career decisions. If you have already made a career decision or are staying in a field in which you have been employed for several years, informational interviewing is inappropriate. In fact, many professionals will be annoyed if you ask them for an informational interview when you are really job seeking. Nevertheless, informational interviews can help you make career decisions and find employment if you are the right person, in the right place at the fortunate moment. Marcia , a burned out social worker, had just moved to Phoenix and was seeking information and ideas about career options. She had several informational interviews with people in fields that she thought might be interesting, but was disappointed. The fourth interview, a lunch appointment, was different. Marcia and her guest liked each other from the outset and spent three hours at lunch. The woman was impressed by Marcia's background and personality and later offered her a position as lobbyist for the state social workers' association. Had the job been advertised in local papers, there would have been several hundred applications and little chance of Marcia even obtaining an interview.

Informational interviews are usually very enjoyable to the interviewee. How often do they have a chance to tell others about their work? It is like giving them an hour of free counseling. Compile a list of questions to ask rather than just saying "tell me about your work." Some good questions include the following:

1. What type of education and training is best for a person entering this type of position?
2. How did you get started in this field?
3. What do you like best and least about the position?
4. What are some of the latest techniques, technology and issues in this career?
5. What is the best way to find employment in this career?
6. What organizations might be hiring in the next year?
7. Does this work allow time for outside interests?

Informational interviews can be set up by phone or letter. Make sure that you tell the person you are not job seeking but rather trying to clarify career directions for yourself. Also communicate the extremely valuable information and advice that this individual can offer you.

Informational interviewing, networking and taking your candidacy to an employer take more time and courage than waiting for an employer to announce a job opening. What these three techniques do though is give individuals more control of their job search by being the initiator rather than passive receiver. Nothing is more frustrating and lonely than waiting for the phone to ring or vacancies to occur. On the other hand, a feeling of moving ahead will be obtained if you take an active approach to job seeking.

CAREER SEARCH STRATEGIES AND PERSONALITY

No one approach to finding a job works well for everyone. People feel comfortable with different techniques. If you are a very outgoing person talking to people and brainstorming options may feel best. If you are more reserved, write down ideas and research options in a career library. If you like to make decisions logically, apply a systematic analysis of organizations and how your skills would fit in with them. Also make checklists and set concrete goals. If you are a creative person, try developing new positions that fit an organizations' needs or develop new work options.

Overcoming Discouragement

If you have tried all of the suggestions above but are not successful in obtaining interviews and job offers, use the following exercises to help with discouragement.

- **Positive Visualization.** Often, when we get a few rejections, we think that no one will ever hire us. Try imagining that people really want to hire you but you have just not found them yet. Visualize their being impressed by your skills and experiences, talking very positively about you and offering you a position. Also visualize your success in previous jobs and remember the praise received from supervisors.

- **Accepting Smaller Successes.** Many people see the job search as an all or nothing situation (e.g. getting a job or failure) rather than small successes. Try to see your progress in smaller steps. Some significant "on the way accomplishments" could include improving your resume, making new contacts, discovering information on employers, or improving your interviewing skills, etc. These successes are extremely important smaller steps toward your major objective and should be recognized.

- **Challenge Your Assumptions.** Often job seekers blame themselves for not finding employment. Look at what you are saying to yourself and see if there are other possible reasons such as a poor economy. Unchallenged negative beliefs can damage your self concept and confidence.

- **Stress Reduction.** As stress builds or job seeking energy dissipates, make sure you take breaks in your job search. Exercise, go to movies, travel or do whatever is needed to reduce your stress level.

Additional Resources

Careers for Book Worms and Other Literary Types. M. Eberts and M. Gisler. VGM Career Horizons.

Careers for Culture Lovers and Other Artsy Types. M. Eberts and M. Gisler. VGM Career Horizons.

Educator's Guide to Alternative Jobs and Careers. Ronald L. Krannich. Impact Publications.

Getting the Job You Really Want. J. Michael Farr. Jist Publications.

Green at Work. Susan Cohen, Island Press.

Guerilla Tactics in the Job Market. Tom Jackson. Bantam Books.

High Impact Telephone Networking for Job Hunters. Howard Armstrong. Bob Adams, Inc.

Jobs for English Majors and Other Smart People. John Munschauer. Peterson's Guides.

Jobs for Travel Buffs and Other Restless Types. Paul Plawin. VGM Career Horizons.

Job Search: The Total System. Dawson & Dawson. John Wiley and Sons.

Knock 'Em Dead with Great Answers to Tough Interview Questions. Martin Yate. Bob Adams, Inc.

Network Your Way to Job and Career Success. Ronald L. Krannich and Caryl R. Krannich. Impact Publications.

The Complete Guide to Public Employment. Ronald L. Krannich and Caryl R. Krannich. Impact Publications,

The Complete Job Search Handbook. Howard Figler. Henry Holt and Co.

The Perfect Resume. Tom Jackson. Doubleday.

The 1993 What Color Is Your Parachute. Richard Bolles. Ten Speed Press, 1993.

111 Proven Techniques and Strategies for Getting the Job Interview. Burdette Bostwick. John Wiley and Sons.

16

POWER, PRESTIGE AND SECURITY

*M*any personal needs are seemingly met through successful careers including power, status, and security. Although it may appear that these needs are being constantly met, there is a tremendous amount of fluctuation even with the most successful professionals. Individuals in charge of a department or division have power only until they make a few bad decisions. Presidents of major corporations have tremendous status until they get fired, which often happens only a few years after hiring. Professionals have a great deal of security until reorganizations or buy-outs occur, and then security disappears. Two messages are observed in these situations. First, long term power, prestige and security are myths, particularly in our rapidly changing society. Second, if you want long term power, prestige and security, **seek them outside of your career.**

POWER

Many individuals strive for power within their organization but very few actually obtain and maintain it. This primarily is due to competition for power from endless numbers of others in organizations. How can this sense of power be obtained outside of your work?

Owning Your Own Business

No matter how large or small, every professional needs to have something they can call their own. This can range from a small consulting or training firm to a part time business. The responsibility, planning, and decision making skills developed will carry over to permanent positions and make us better employees. Individual tolerance will increase due to power needs being met elsewhere.

Politics

Whether it be as member of the school board or a local political office, politics or anti-politics offer constant opportunity to exercise power. Coalition groups must be formed in these situations for survival without severe trauma.

Controlling Diet

Believe it or not, until we have power over our impulses, it is difficult to have power over anyone else. Try controlling your diet for two days and you will experience much greater confidence for power over others. Imagine that cookie or cheeseburger to be someone who is asking you to perform something of displeasure and reject the demand. You will feel more power instantly.

Weight Lifting

Many adults and elderly over the past several years have taken up weight lifting. Added muscle strength gives individuals increased sense of psychological well being and power. Consult a personal trainer for proper techniques before engaging in weight training.

Automobiles

As America's power in the world has diminished, so has the size and power of the automobiles we drive. When you step on the gas pedal of your car does it accelerate like a turtle? If so, you are denying yourself a source of power that can make you feel better about your life. Also, try driving a vehicle that is higher off the ground and you will have a sense of power over those "small guys."

Assertiveness Everyday

Often we lose a sense of power because of lack of assertiveness in everyday interactions. Take an assertiveness class and review chapter five in this book for assertiveness suggestions.

Other Sources of Power

Horseback riding
Dog training

How can you increase power in your life?

1. _____
2. _____
3. _____

PRESTIGE

Almost everyone likes prestige and recognition to one degree or another. Prestige can mean having many friends or being world renowned. Self esteem is boosted by prestige and recognition. If you are in a high visibility position at work, or in a professional position such as a doctor or judge, prestige will come automatically. Most occupations these days have very little prestige, primarily due to media disclosure of the negative aspects of the positions. Lawyers, politicians, professional athletes, bankers, and numerous other occupations were revered between 1950 and 1970. These days they are looked upon, at best, as normal people with the same faults as everyone else.

How can you obtain prestige and recognition outside of your work?

Part Time Teaching

Teaching elementary, college students or adults, either part time or as a guest lecturer, will increase prestige. Sometimes you may even impress yourself with what you know. Contact high schools, specific academic departments within colleges and/or career service offices and they will usually welcome you. High school and junior high students are usually more difficult to impress and you may end up the learner.

Mentoring

Many individuals ages 10-40 are looking for mentors. Your experience, ideas and wisdom can provide essential support for their growth and development. What's in it for you? Not only can you help an individual with their life, but your peers will respect you more.

Association Offices

Professional associations are frequently seeking individuals to fill official positions from president to membership chair. Your peers, spouse and members in the organization will be impressed by your position. Additionally you can network to find employment, increase understanding of issues in the field, and develop new skills. What is the worst office in professional associations? The treasurer is the worst because of hard work, constant problems and lack of recognition.

Writing Articles

Thousands of newspapers, magazines, newsletters and other publications are in dire need of articles in a wide range of topics. Most of us have knowledge in several areas that would be useful to others. Visit your local library and you may be amazed at the number of publications that exist.

Professional Presentations

Professional organizations hold weekly, monthly and yearly meetings in which one to two hour presentations are given. If you dislike being on stage by yourself, get a panel together and/or solicit group interaction and the pressure will decrease.

Fund Raising

Social service programs, health issues, arts causes and many other groups have fund raisers throughout the year. Volunteer at these events and your prestige and self esteem will increase.

Start a Non-Profit Organization

There are many issues in our society that are unresolved. Non-profit organizations work on issues related to the environment, animals, child care, families, education, ethics and hundreds of other areas. If an issue is not addressed by a non-profit organization in your area, start an association. You may be surprised that other individuals in your area will join you once goals and activities are organized. For assistance on developing a non-profit organization, contact your local chamber of commerce.

SECURITY

Security is something we all seek but is difficult to find, particularly in a society like ours that changes so rapidly. Even in Japan, lifetime employment in a company is no longer guaranteed. Actually this was a myth that only 10 to 25 percent of Japanese achieved. If you want real security, help others deal with their insecurities and you will always be busy. The employment outlook for psychologists is excellent.

Since employment security is diminishing, how can we obtain it through other areas of our lives?

Savings

Americans have savings phobia and need instant gratification. Try saving money at least four times a week when you would have spent it for lunches, unneeded entertainment or other impulsive acts. Other money wasters include automobiles, clothes, and excessive use of credit cards.

Investments

A good financial planner can earn you many times what they cost. Many Americans have money invested in areas with very low return.

Friendships

Security is greatly enhanced by friendship. Try to maintain many people in your "friendship savings account."

Relatives

Most people have love/hate relationships with their relatives. Past disagreements overshadow the love that really exists. When times get tough though, most of our relatives will help out. Try reconnecting with relatives if you have lost contact with them and talk about good memories.

Personal Health

When our health is poor, security quickly begins to crumble, regardless of the stability of our employer. It is crucial that we each take responsibility for our health and do what is necessary to maintain it. Recent studies show that our immune system is bolstered by exercise, rest, non-smoking, good diet such as non-fatty foods, and taking vitamin C, E, and Beta Carotene.

Health Care

Health care is rapidly changing in the U.S. Many individuals fear losing the medical benefits provided by their employer. If proposed legislation passes, the government will guarantee individual health care coverage regardless of one's employer or employment status. This will make it much easier for individuals to change employers and start their own businesses.

Retirement

Individuals expecting social security to fulfill their retirement needs are in for a rude awakening. With the numbers of elderly increasing each year, social security may go bankrupt early next century. Benefits may be reduced. What can we do? We all must start retirement savings as young as possible. This means no later than our early forties. Also many people are retirement poor but house wealthy. If you are one of them, consider selling your house and moving somewhere less expensive to live.

Relax

Inability to relax causes many problems in our society. Most Americans are constantly on the go. Is this constant motion caused by our insecurity or merely feeding it? Regardless, if we can relax we will feel more secure, have more energy to deal the real issues, and refrain from spending unnecessary money.

Think Positive

A large part of security is psychological not material. If we can think positively, more secure outcomes will occur. Try to imagine what your ideal security in life would be and visualize yourself already there. Frequently this visualization is better than the reality anyway. What can you do **now** for your current security.

Find the Joy in Little Things

How often have you expected a vacation, new car, summer home, family reunion, or Christmas holiday to be outstanding, only to be disappointed. Often we overlook obvious little things that could make us feel secure. Looking at a flower, listening to some peaceful music, taking a slow walk, relaxing with a hot bath are activities that can increase security feelings. Try to develop the habit of doing at least one of these a day for your security and peace of mind.

References

Building Wealth. Russ Whitney. Simon & Schuster, 1994.

Control Your Destiny or Someone Else Will. Noel Tichy. Harper, 1994.

How to Pay Zero Taxes. Jeff Schnepper. McGraw Hill, 1994.

Money Smart. Ester Berger. Simon & Schuster, 1993.

The Wealthy Barber. David Chilton. Prima Press, 1993.

21st Century Leadership: Dialogues With 100 Top Leaders. Lynn McFarland. Leadership Press, 1993.

Unlimited Power. Anthony Robbins. Fawcett, 1986.

Women in Power. Dorothy Cantor. Houghton-Mifflin, 1992.

17

MAKING THE LEAP TO SUCCESS

*S*andra was watching ships move through locks at the canal several months ago in Seattle. One little tug boat was pulling a huge barge with logs weighing several times its own weight. When it came time for the tug boat to move through the locks, several minutes of pushing the engine at near full throttle was necessary to get moving forward. The experienced tug boat captain was very patient and in control the whole time. Similarly, it may take a while to build up enough steam to get going in your new success directions. Most people need a minimum of three months to feel real successes. If you develop the skills outlined earlier and combine them with your goals and support from others, your new life style will be easier to achieve. Making all changes at once will be difficult, therefore try to think long range. Consider success as a life-long project and ease yourself into this new world.

SUCCESS OBJECTIVES CONTRACT

After deciding on areas for development, you are moving towards success. What remains will involve putting decisions into action. One useful tool to facilitate action is the **Success Objectives Contract**. This document is an agreement between yourself and significant others that you will agree to work on predetermined success goals. Complete the sections below and have the contract signed by one director of your success committee and a peer. These contracts can span whatever time you desire but should initially not exceed two months. Subsequently other contracts can be drawn up with different time spans or goals. Give copies of your contract to the two people signing it and meet with them at least twice a month for input and suggestions.

The contract contains sections on goals, activities to achieve them, people who can help you, evaluation and rewards. Additionally there are statements about your responsibilities and those of the other signees.

Success Objectives Contract

Name:
Address:
Phone:
Dates of Contract: From_____ To_____
Success Goal for Time Period:

1. _____
2. _____
3. _____

What activities will be conducted to achieve goals and when.

Activity	**Time Frame**
1. _____	_____
2. _____	_____
3. _____	_____

People who can help you.

1. _____
2. _____
3. _____

Evaluation of progress; how will you know if you are moving towards your goals?

Rewards for yourself.

1. _____
2. _____
3. _____

Signatures:

You_____ Date_____

Your responsibility is to fulfill the contract to the best of your ability and seek assistance when necessary.

Peer_____ Date_____

Peer responsibility is to help you complete the contract on agreed upon methods.

Director _____ Date_____

Board of Director member responsibility is to provide feedback and suggestions on achieving the goals.

SETTING UP A SUCCESS SCHEDULE

Success schedules look different than regular work schedules. Regular work schedules are packed tight with meetings, appointments, and deadlines. Success schedules look something like the one below and have more flow, exercise, relaxation and learning. The ? indicates time to do whatever you want. Set up your own schedule for next week and modify it for following weeks until the combination that is most successful for you develops.

Success Schedule

	Mon.	Tues.	Wed.	Thurs.	Fri.	Sat.	Sun.
8	exercise	class	work	class	work	?	family
9	work	class	work	class	work	?	family
10	work	work	work	relax	work	?	family
11	work	work	work	relax	work	?	family
12	social	exercise	work	exercise	relax	?	family
1	work	?	exercise	work	relax	?	friend
2	work	?	read	work	relax	?	friend
3	work	?	read	work	relax	?	friend
4	read	?	read	work	relax	?	friend
5	read	?	read	relax	social	?	family
6	relax	?	social	relax	social	?	family
7	relax	social	?	exercise	social	?	family
8	relax	social	?	exercise	social	?	family
9	relax	social	?	relax	relax	?	family

Learning from Each Day

Successful people constantly learn from their experiences and make appropriate changes. Particularly during this growth stage of your life, reflect on what you did and learned each day. Review each day for:

- What went well?
- What could have been done better?
- What you learned.
- What you will do to make it better?

Fast or Slow Change

How quickly would you prefer to make changes in your life? Most of us prefer instant change which, of course, is unrealistic. Additionally, rapid change is usually superficial and does not last long. Change is a function of three factors; time, energy and resources. If you have a great deal of these, new successes may come very quickly. On the other hand, if these are scarce, changes occur more slowly. It is wise not to force change too quickly because frustration and exhaustion occur. Set your goals for the next six months rather than one month or five years. Six months should give you adequate time to deal with barriers, develop resources, create a support group and enact modifications. If you use strategies outlined in this book, in six months significant changes should occur. Good luck and let me know what happens.

Additional Resources

Do It. John-Roger & Peter McWilliams. Prelude Press, 1991.

Doing It Now. Edwin C. Bliss. Bantam Books, 1976.

Getting Things Done. Edwin C. Bliss, Bantam Books, 1984.

INDEX

CAREER
RESOURCES

Contact Impact Publications to receive a free copy of their latest comprehensive and annotated catalog of over 2,000 career resources (books, subscriptions, training programs, videos, audiocassettes, computer software, and CD-ROM).

The following career resources are available directly from Impact Publications. Complete the following form or list the titles, include postage (see formula at the end), enclose payment, and send your order along with your name and address to:

IMPACT PUBLICATIONS
9104-N Manassas Drive
Manassas Park, VA 22111
Tel. 703/361-7300
FAX 703/335-9486

Orders from individuals must be prepaid by check, moneyorder, Visa or MasterCard number. We accept telephone and FAX orders with a Visa or MasterCard number.

Qty.	TITLES	Price	TOTAL
JOBS AND CAREERS			
___	Change Your Job, Change Your Life	$14.95	___
___	Complete Job Finder's Guide to the 90s	$13.95	___
___	Cracking the Over-50 Job Market	$11.95	___
___	Dynamite Tele-Search	$10.95	___
___	Electronic Job Search Revolution	$12.95	___
___	Five Secrets to Finding a Job	$12.95	___

__ How to Get Interviews From Classified Job Ads	$14.95	_____
__ How to Succeed Without a Career Path	$13.95	_____
__ Professional's Job Finder	$18.95	_____
__ Rites of Passage At $100,000+	$29.95	_____

SKILLS, TESTING, SELF-ASSESSMENT, EMPOWERMENT

__ 7 Habits of Highly Effective People	$11.00	_____
__ Discover the Best Jobs for You	$11.95	_____
__ Do What You Are	$14.95	_____
__ Do What You Love, the Money Will Follow	$10.95	_____
__ Finding the Hat That Fits	$10.00	_____
__ Stop Postponing the Rest of Your Life	$9.95	_____
__ Where Do I Go From Here With My Life?	$10.95	_____
__ Wishcraft	$10.95	_____

RESUMES AND LETTERS

__ Dynamite Cover Letters	$10.95	_____
__ Dynamite Resumes	$10.95	_____
__ Electronic Resumes for the New Job Market	$11.95	_____
__ High Impact Resumes and Letters	$12.95	_____
__ Job Search Letters That Get Results	$12.95	_____
__ The Resume Catalog	$15.95	_____
__ Resumes for Re-Entry	$10.95	_____

INTERVIEWS, NETWORKING & SALARY NEGOTIATIONS

__ 60 Seconds and You're Hired!	$9.95	_____
__ Dynamite Answers to Interview Questions	$10.95	_____
__ Dynamite Salary Negotiation	$12.95	_____
__ Great Connections	$11.95	_____
__ How to Work a Room	$9.95	_____
__ Interview for Success	$11.95	_____
__ New Network Your Way to Job and Career Success	$12.95	_____
__ The Secrets of Savvy Networking	$11.99	_____

DRESS, APPEARANCE, IMAGE

__ John Molloy's New Dress for Success (men)	$10.95	_____
__ Red Socks Don't Work! (men)	$14.95	_____
__ The Winning Image	$17.95	_____

BEST JOBS AND EMPLOYERS FOR THE 90s

__ 100 Best Companies to Work for in America	$27.95	_____
__ 100 Best Jobs for the 1990s and Beyond	$19.95	_____
__ 101 Careers	$12.95	_____
__ American Almanac of Jobs and Salaries	$17.00	_____
__ America's 50 Fastest Growing Jobs	$9.95	_____
__ America's Fastest Growing Employers	$14.95	_____
__ Best Jobs for the 1990s and Into the 21st Century	$12.95	_____
__ Job Seeker's Guide to 1000 Top Employers	$22.95	_____

___ Jobs 1994 $15.95 ___
___ New Emerging Careers $14.95 ___
___ Top Professions $10.95 ___

KEY DIRECTORIES

___ American Salaries and Wages Survey $94.95 ___
___ Career Training Sourcebook $24.95 ___
___ Complete Guide for Occupational Exploration $29.95 ___
___ Dictionary of Occupational Titles $39.95 ___
___ Directory of Executive Recruiters (annual) $39.95 ___
___ Encyclopedia of Careers and Vocational Guidance $129.95 ___
___ Enhanced Guide for Occupational Exploration $29.95 ___
___ Internships (annual) $29.95 ___
___ Job Bank Guide to Employment Services (annual) $149.95 ___
___ Job Hunter's Sourcebook $59.95 ___
___ Moving and Relocation Directory $149.00 ___
___ National Directory of Addresses & Telephone Numbers $129.95 ___
___ National Job Bank (annual) $249.95 ___
___ National Trade and Professional Associations $79.95 ___
___ Occupational Outlook Handbook $22.95 ___
___ Personnel Executives Contactbook $149.00 ___
___ Places Rated Almanac $21.95 ___
___ Professional Careers Sourcebook $79.95 ___

ALTERNATIVE JOBS AND CAREERS

___ Adventure Careers $9.95 ___
___ Advertising Career Directory $17.95 ___
___ Business and Finance Career Directory $17.95 ___
___ But What If I Don't Want to Go to College? $10.95 ___
___ Career Opportunities in the Music Industry $27.95 ___
___ Careers for Animal Lovers $12.95 ___
___ Careers for Nature Lovers $12.95 ___
___ Careers for Numbers Crunchers $12.95 ___
___ Careers for Sports Nuts $12.95 ___
___ Careers for Travel Buffs $12.95 ___
___ Careers in Computers $16.95 ___
___ Careers in Health Care $16.95 ___
___ Careers in Medicine $16.95 ___
___ Careers in the Outdoors $12.95 ___
___ Environmental Career Guide $14.95 ___
___ Health Care Job Explosion $14.95 ___
___ Opportunities in Computer Science $13.95 ___
___ Opportunities in Law $13.95 ___
___ Opportunities in Medical Technology $13.95 ___
___ Travel and Hospitality Career Directory $17.95 ___

INTERNATIONAL, OVERSEAS, AND TRAVEL JOBS

___ Almanac of International Jobs and Careers $19.95 ___
___ Complete Guide to International Jobs & Careers $13.95 ___
___ Guide to Careers in World Affairs $14.95 ___

__ Jobs for People Who Love Travel $12.95 _____
__ Jobs in Russia and the Newly Independent States $15.95 _____

PUBLIC-ORIENTED CAREERS

__ Almanac of American Government Jobs and Careers $14.95 _____
__ Complete Guide to Public Employment $19.95 _____
__ Find a Federal Job Fast! $13.95 _____
__ Government Job Finder $14.95 _____
__ Jobs and Careers With Nonprofit Organizations $14.95 _____

ENTREPRENEURSHIP AND SELF-EMPLOYMENT

__ 101 Best Businesses to Start $15.00 _____
__ Best Home-Based Businesses for the 90s $10.95 _____
__ Entrepreneur's Guide to Starting a Successful Business $16.95 _____
__ Have You Got What It Takes? $12.95 _____

           SUBTOTAL   _____

Virginia residents add 4½% sales tax   _____

POSTAGE/HANDLING ($4.00 for first
title and $1.00 for each additional book) $4.00
Number of additional titles x $1.00 ----------
TOTAL ENCLOSED ----------------- _____

SHIP TO:

NAME _____

ADDRESS _____

_____

_____

[ ] I enclose check/moneyorder for $ _____ made
     payable to IMPACT PUBLICATIONS.

[ ] Please charge $ _____ to my credit card:

     Card # _____

     Expiration date: _____/_____

     Signature _____